Lourdes
Healing and Rebirth

Lourdes
Healing and Rebirth

August 5, 2024 (handwritten)

Sophie Delay
Photographer

Preface by
Thierry Hubert

Translated by
Anne Englund Nash

IGNATIUS PRESS   SAN FRANCISCO

Original French edition:
Lourdes, guérir et renaître
© 2021 Les Éditions du Cerf: Paris

Art Design and pictures © Sophie Delay

© 2023 by Ignatius Press, San Francisco
ISBN 978-1-62164-576-4
Library of Congress Catalogue number 2022940075
Printed in Canada ∞

CONTENTS

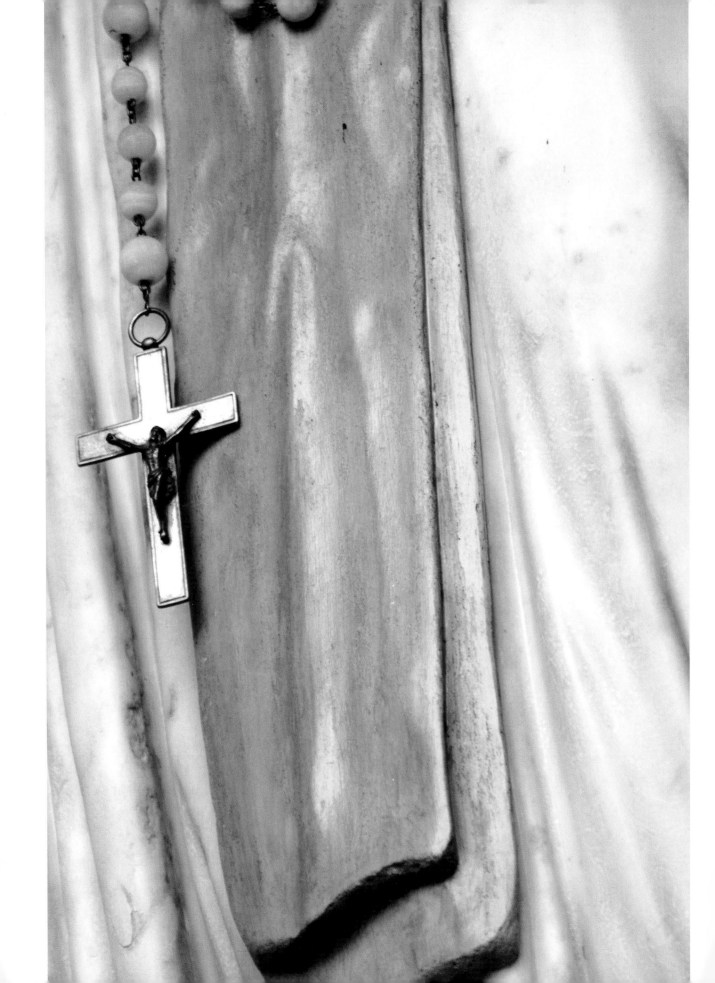

A LITTLE CORNER OF HEAVEN ON A LITTLE PIECE OF LAND

Thierry Hubert

December 8, 2020, on the Feast of the Immaculate Conception

I love Lourdes. But it was not easy. Lots of bad pictures, coming from Sulpician images, cynical conversations, and haughty judgments had built up almost everywhere in my head, in my heart, and in my body. Lourdes? Just the residue of a religious faith from a nineteenth-century past, a survival of apparitions and miracles that, as a young man, admittedly Catholic, but presumably modern and scientific, I had to brush aside. "Stupid masquerades and a shameful exploitation of peoples' credulity", could be read in the local newspaper in Lourdes at the time of the apparitions. The case seemed to be closed. Was it then the little trickle of joy, like the one from the rock, heard in the voices of some friends who went there every year, that made me agree to accompany them in order to see? It was necessary for me to be magnetized by the joy. In order to bring down

the mountains of pride, I had to discover the hollow of a lost valley in the Pyrenees. To learn to serve, bend my body, and to receive strength from the sick. To get back up from my falls, to be plunged into the water of the pool. One does not leave Lourdes unscathed. One leaves it living and loving, even the first time. The years that have elapsed since have taught me, after I became religious, to discover the beauty of this little corner of heaven on a little piece of earth. I love Lourdes.

I love Lourdes because there is no need to be in good standing in order to go there. When the Church very quickly departs from very high, much too high, conditions in order to be able to be a part of her family here at Lourdes, the doors are opened. No one asks you for an adequate profession of faith or even a certificate of

11

baptism; anybody can enter and go to the blessed grotto. Those who flock there are, besides, just ordinary people. It may well be that some great ones slip in, but they most often remain anonymous, as the masks of success find no place here. The sole desire to approach a mystery and to be able to dwell in it are enough. A strange crowd where you have, side by side, one with a rosary in hand and one with nose piercings,

pilgrims from the villages and foreigners from all continents, the devout and the unfaithful, the one who believes in heaven and the one who does not, but all, nevertheless, desire very secretly to be touched. Only to be there, in order to see, hidden near a tree or behind a pillar of the basilica, seated in front of the grotto or before the lighted candles, always in search of silence. In order to be there in Lourdes, it is best

"*I love*

not to miss it yourself. And to give yourself—or perhaps finally to receive—the grace of being present. Really present. "Do you want to do me the favor of coming here?", the Woman in the hollow of the rock whispers to us again today.

I love Lourdes because the miracle is permanent there. I mean the miracle of conversion, of passage. It would be wrong to think that only the sick come here necessarily with the hope of recovering from illness. The permanent miracle of Lourdes is that of the peace that is deposited in the anguished heart. The rock that is broken open lets the grotto appear. In the cavity nestles the beautiful Lady, and at her feet flows, buried, the water from the spring. From our hearts, hardened by a life that does not always spare us, by too abrupt a destiny, Life can also resurge. To approach the grotto is to lead my body to the place where faith gives me hope: a life that is more alive, that flows from heaven, a life that makes the Kingdom of heaven visible, a life that can be tasted even now, already in the present. "I do not promise to make you happy in this world, but in the other", the Lady said one day to a young shepherdess. What has not been said of this "other world" that would only be the reward for a life of misery on the day of her death? For a long time, I could not stand these words. I understood their meaning by watching the totally happy caregivers serve their sick brothers and sisters. The other world is within reach of your heart and your hands when you open yourself to the unexpected from the Spirit, when you begin to be servants. The other world, Eternal Life, is for the one who

She raises herself to just the right height, ours, and tells us that in heaven, the language of every person is spoken. As for me, who am not a foreign language ace, that is a cause for rejoicing! The art of being multilingual, though so useful in the sanctuary, finds a happy resolution in the heart that is open to prayer. My vocabulary and grammatical mistakes are not an obstacle. She, the beautiful Lady, makes it

Lourdes "

loves or who already desires to love, when to live on love still seems too distant or too inaccessible. I love Lourdes, in order to see what, elsewhere, is no longer seen in fact.

I love Lourdes because this Lady chooses as a holiday resort a lost space of a lost village on a little piece of not very accessible land, between muddy waters and a forest of bushes on the side of a rock. "The Virgin at Massabielle? We lead pigs there! Thus gossiped the gossips", the annals reported. The wisdom of God is folly for men…. and His mother, no doubt, made good use of it. Far from cities and drawing rooms, far from self-righteous places and worldly customs, the Lady lives here. Certainly that suits her well, for she loved to smile. But there is still more. The beautiful Lady speaks the young Bernadette's local dialect: "Que soy era Immaculada Counceptiou" (I am the Immaculate Conception) will be confided to her on March 25, on the feast of the Annunciation. That Mary, who is proclaimed the Queen of Heaven, rises to the language of the little people, of those who have no knowledge of the realm of fine-talking, is very powerful. She does not lower herself, either out of condescension or out of humility.

her own business. She even gives us her name in that language in order to give us a reflection of our own identity. She, who is spotless, tells us again what we knew but what we had perhaps forgotten. She tells us again that all our imperfections—let us call this our sin—injure us and wound our humanity. We are not reducible to our flawed actions. She, the Immaculate Conception, tells us that God's dream has already been realized for each one of us. The Lady is beautiful, and we are beautiful, with

that beauty of the children of God. On the day of her second visit to Massabielle, "Bernadette says: 'There is a light! There it is!'", notes one of her biographers, Marcelle Auclair. There we are, we could say, essentially luminous. This is what we celebrate in the end, without being too aware of it, in the evening, in the streets of the town above or in the sanctuary below, with our lighted candles, in a procession like a parade in which each illumined face is a sign of this beauty. Together we form but a single

luminous body that moves behind Mary, the first one on this path, in order to lead us to the foot of the basilica and to the foot of her Son. In the Gospels as here in the sanctuary, Mary is, actually, much more discreet than one might think. Lourdes, a Marian shrine? Certainly, but it is Jesus who is shown. His word is offered and his body shared "for the life of the world". His Eucharistic Body, every afternoon, opens the procession and is exposed. The two bodies—the risen body present under the modest appearance of the bread, and the body of the people gathered there—actually form only one.

I love Lourdes because the sick are not the sick. That is still not the least of the reversals. For if we love to say that the sick have the first place here and that they are pampered—and that, of course, is true—I also suspect, a suspicion several times confirmed, that in the mystery of their illnesses and handicaps, they contribute as much, and indeed much more, than they

François

(Prénom de l'intéressé)

PAR CETTE ONCTION SAINTE,
QUE LE SEIGNEUR,
EN SA GRANDE BONTÉ,
VOUS RÉCONFORTE

“ *Transparent to grace,*
the sick mend the
apparently healthy ones
that we are. ”

COIFFES

receive. Transparent to grace, the sick mend the apparently healthy ones that we are. Their whispered words, an aside from a conversation that one would otherwise judge too quickly to be insignificant, have the power of an essential word, living and creative. Their glances penetrate without judgment the winding and congested roads of a weary and rigid heart. Many of those who approach them say they receive a lesson in life. Not that we have to silence our own suffering in the face of the still greater suffering of the sick. But we understand thereby that the lesson is an indication of a passage of a Passover, of a recovery, of a laborious and humble reconnection. The sick are the true actors at Lourdes. They make the Gospel real, they are the messengers, even if silent, who carry the good news of a salvation for all. I will even go farther. By learning to approach the sick, to win them over, to take care of them, and to cherish them, it is our own illnesses and handicaps that we are learning to approach, to win over, and to cherish. The sick learn to love themselves, in short; and better to love their neighbor as themselves. The free service at Lourdes effectively provides a good return on investment.

I love Lourdes because holiness is at the edge of the water and close to the meadows. Bernadette obviously left her mark, which has since had followers. Paul Claudel, in his litanies, would be able to describe it: "limpid shepherdess, drop of water from the Gave, intrepid and pure eye, servant of azure!" So here is this little bit of a little girl who, with Thérèse, several years later in Lisieux, would revolutionize the Church. Their way of living their trust in God, each pursuing her singular little way, would give back a youthfulness to their Church, paralyzed in practices marked by a scrupulous Jansenism. The child of Lourdes is direct and simple, which is to say, uncomplicated. Limpid as the water from the rock, once the mud has been cleared. To those very serious gentlemen in ecclesiastical robes, who wanted, in all good faith, to trap her and prove deception, she replies: "I am not responsible for making you believe it; I am responsible for telling it to you!" A marvelous gift of strength that overthrows the powerful. The Magnificat is read here and everywhere in shrines. Generations proclaim Mary blessed, and to the most humble, the Mighty works miracles. The Beatitudes have also found, at every side of the Gave, space for application: "Blessed are the pure of heart, blessed are the thirsty, blessed are the merciful!"

I love Lourdes because joy floods and overflows there. The Gave, sometimes jealous and furious, tries to bypass it anyway, but certainly without ever succeeding. In all periods, for more than 160 years, the same observation applies as was given by Cardinal Pacelli, who came from Rome in 1935: "never in any place on earth has one seen such a procession of suffering, never such radiance of peace, serenity, and joy". Rarely, in fact, over so large an area, are misery and suffering shown and displayed to this point. There would be enough there to divert one's gaze, to fall still farther down

Thierry Hubert

Thierry Hubert is a Dominican and producer of the *Jour du Seigneur* [which provides access to Mass on television and the Internet, etc.].

into sadness and despair, swept away and overwhelmed by this human tide of pain and deformed bodies. How can joy then make its home there without crushing still more those who seem to be excluded? Perhaps everything is determined by touch. By the hands of a hospital worker who tenderly wraps the cramped body of a cold old man in a knitted blanket. By the raised hand of the confessor who forgives the sinner for what he had never dared to say, kept captive in the shadows. By the arms of the swimming pool attendant, accompanying the body of the pilgrim, plunged into and then raised from death as from his coffin. By the arms of the father carrying his sick child close to him and who finally takes charge of him, touches him, and lives this moment like a second birth. Hands touching a face, kisses offered as thanksgiving. At Lourdes, heaven meets the earth, love and truth embrace. Joy is perhaps also shown, deepened more profoundly, by faith, which is capable of moving mountains and crowds, capable of transforming all these anonymous people into a community of brothers and sisters, friends confident of meeting and finding each other again. This faith is nourished, every day, by the pilgrimage, by the Bread from Heaven shared by the multitude, becoming then the Body of the resurrected Christ. This faith carries and supports the weight of the day, of every day. "Faith is already bread. It helps one eat the black bread; it helps one wait, patiently, past the hour when it was supposed to come", wrote Louis Veuillot. Joy is in the superabundance revealed by a life in excess, even in the dark days of crucifixion. It is born, stunned by the unexpected confidence that all the forces of death will not have the last word.

This joy is palpable at Lourdes and floats above the shrine. It covers the pilgrim and the curious. Mysteriously, it obliges each one, without, however, forcing him, to take a little sidestep in order to depart from his too-well-drawn straight line, to cause in that way a change of perspective and to discover then charity in action, right beside him. Joy, joy, joy!

And yet, Lourdes has fallen silent. Or nearly so, during this whole year of 2020, in these months when the COVID-19 pandemic was striking and spreading its web across all the continents. Not one sick person in the reception areas of Saint-Frai and Notre-Dame, no more long processions gathering up to 20,000 pilgrims, no more long lines waiting for the baths, no more stations of the cross on the mountain. Only a few individual pilgrims or diocesan or national pilgrimage delegations between two lockdowns in order to mark symbolically the visceral attachment of everyone to this little corner of heaven. Then, in order to get through this unprecedented crisis, Lourdes has reinvented itself. Since the pilgrims can no longer come to the grotto, it is the grotto that has come to them, through small digital screens. The Virgin and Bernadette, in a few clicks. Every day, morning Mass and the afternoon rosary have gathered all over the world hundreds of thousands of prayers, forming an invisible communion, bearing in these troubled and distressing times the anxiety of the world. An unbroken chain of prayers, in the secrecy of a room or cell, of a living room or a little chapel, has borne the concern of our humanity by entrusting it to the One who remains, in every generation, the consoler of the afflicted, the sweet refuge in this valley of tears. In these days of anxiety, Lourdes has not let us down. Bernadette, like her fellow saint Thérèse of Lisieux, does in fact "spend her heaven doing good on earth".

" *Joy, joy, joy!* "

This very beautiful book would like to continue the adventure: to visit Lourdes from what has been said or written since the time of the apparitions, augmented by magnificent photos from a photographer in love with the place, Sophie Delay.

When you read it and contemplate the images, I invite you to hold this book in your hands as if it were a little piece of that land visited by heaven. From page to page, I invite you to let yourself be surprised, to whisper a Hail Mary, to let yourself be moved, or to perceive your heart beating more joyously. Perhaps you will feel the stirrings of a new desire to go there, to see … and all the rest will be grace.

OPENING

PANORAMA OF LOURDES

Joris-Karl Huysmans

Les foules de Lourdes [The Crowds at Lourdes], 1906

This morning, it is raining like it rains in this country, which is to say, in buckets; and, seated close to the window of the cottage where I live, at the top of the Pau road, I am looking at the panorama of Lourdes through my weeping window panes.

The horizon, which is very short, is disrupted by mountains, between which rise tufts of white vapor, while at higher altitudes charcoal black clouds speed by and sooty flakes from factories roll by. The top of one of these mountains looks like it is smoking, while the peak of another, freed from its clouds, seems dead; here and there, grey cotton scarves wrap around the neck of the lowest hills and spread out as they descend; as for the cones whose heads are eternally whitened by the snow, they have completely disappeared in the mist; to the degree that rains fall, everything is blurred; the great and the small Gers, the two closest mountains, resemble, in this mist, immense pyramids of the residue of burned coal, gigantic heaps of ash.

The sadness of this sky striped diagonally by the thread of rain! Below the range of these mountains, just in front of me, the Gave, in a streaming torrent, before extending farther into a tranquil river, encircles with foam a building with a pointed belltower on top of it and surrounded by a narrow garden planted with firs and poplars. It looks like a prison, with that construction pierced, very high up, in very straight walls, by tiny skylights; it is the convent of the Poor Clares; on the left, a bridge spans the river and connects the new Lourdes, whose houses I can see, to the old city, dominated by an ancient fortress that looks as if it were made for an opera setting, with painted canvases; one would think it unreal; finally, on the right, the esplanade with its trees leading to the Rosary and to the double ramp that overlooks the basilica, whose profile stands out, all white, against the Hill of Espélugues, where, to represent the stations of Calvary, enormous crosses stand in clearings surrounded by greenery.

And behind the esplanade and its lawns, at the bottom of the ramps, two gas bells, one, enameled in pale green, the other colored with yellow ochre like a door to places, become round, horrible; one of these sheet-metal pies contains a view of Jerusalem, the other, a view of Lourdes.

All of that is not very captivating from the point of view of art, and neither is the cathedral, perched as well on a strip of rock, in the air. Thin, narrow, without any worthy embellishment, it evokes the miserable memory of those cork churches of which certain industry storefronts adorned themselves. It falls within the aesthetics of a cork merchant; the least of the village chapels, built in the Middle Ages, seems, in comparison to this contraband Gothic, a masterpiece of subtlety and strength; the best part, despite its cold bareness, would be the double stone ramp that leads from the bottom of the esplanade up to its gate if it weren't itself spoiled at its point of arrival by the horrible roof of the Rosary that sticks out under the foot of the basilica, a roof composed of a colossal Savoy cake pan flanked by three boiler covers in zinc.

Seen from where I am, from the side, one would say this rotunda, with its two descending ramps, undulating from its roof to the ground, is like a giant crab whose legs stretch out their claws toward the old city. And, at the bottom of this ramp, under the basilica and along the Rosary, runs, in front of the Gave riverbeds, a large alleyway that passes in front of the pools and the grotto and disappears, suddenly blocked by a hill on which switchbacks are traced in the form of an M. They climb, by paths planted with trees, behind the basilica and lead on to the residence of the Fathers of the Grotto and the episcopal residence situated several steps from the apse.

All that is revealed as ethical and puny, scanty and dwarfed, for the scale of very close mountains crushes it; but the poverty of this prepared setting fades if you look into the fire pit dug into the rock below the basilica itself; it is a cave of flames that burn under its side; what is of interest in Lourdes is there. 🕊

Joris-Karl Huysmans

THE GROTTO

Louis Colin

Le parfum de Lourdes [The Perfume of Lourdes], 1889

The soul! Who will tell us its secrets and its mysteries? It is the sun, and it is the night; it is clear water, and it is the ocean. The soul, high as the heavens; the soul, deep as the infinite! Since it donned the mantle of sin, the soul has yielded to all disguises. Daughter of light, it looks for the night; heaven of purity, it is covered with clouds. The sinful man juggles with his soul as with a common toy. We adorn that with the fine name of human politics.

In the grotto, everything reappears in truth and light. Stripped of all its artifices, the soul is completely naked there, with its weight of miseries and sins. It trembles and it prays, it judges itself and it begs, it feels and it cries. Who could hear its cries without being moved? How true everything is there! How profound everything is there! How good the human barometer is there in its own degree!

No more vanities or bragging or false shame. No more costumes to cover oneself from the eyes of men as from one's own eyes.

It is the truth that speaks, and that truth is earnestly pleading. It is a suffering that moans, a poverty that is torment, a deep night that invokes the light, one in exile who cries for the distant joys of his homeland.

The soul!

It is a valley of tears, seeking to drink the dew of the eternal mountains!

No paintbrush can capture these sublime attitudes, these brilliant eyes, these bowed foreheads, these open arms, or these breasts ready to break. The body of those praying speaks like their soul, and without wanting to, without ever dreaming of it, it takes on all the attitudes of a sovereign eloquence. Art will never equal reality; for, besides moral afflictions, there are also physical afflictions. They are innumerable there. During the national pilgrimage, eight hundred sick people there, and, good God, how many infirmities altogether!

Those with leprosy next to those with cancer, the dwarf, the paralytic, the deformed, the lame, those with mange, the consumptive, the anemic, those with varicose veins, with dropsy, an immense hospital, a book of a thousand pages in which the story of sin unfolds, illustrated by a picture of all human sufferings, of original sin with its procession of sorrows, an embassy at the feet of the Immaculate Conception.

What a spectacle and what compassion! The sick arrive, carried on stretchers or brought on carts. If they represent all infirmities, they also personify all hopes. Before their arrival, the public prayers, through a thousand echoes, give off something triumphant and joyful. These great murmurings of the crowd, which in turn lament, glorify, acclaim, and implore, these uninterrupted supplications, these songs from far and near, that from the north and from the south of France come to beat the foot of the Pyrenees, they are the soul of France, acclaiming without end the Immaculate Mary with Jesus. It is also the cry of the mutilated homeland that walks to the resurrection of itself.

But when the sick make their appearance, the prayers change course; it is for these unfortunate ones that everyone begins to beg Our Lady of Lourdes. The dying are going to be bathed in the pool; they must come out of it healed.

An hour passes in this way. Arms are crossed, foreheads are lowered to the dust, voices are tormented and penetrating. Mary and Jesus are seated in their Grotto; they end up giving in; and suddenly a cry of victory sounds: the Magnificat announces in the distance a cure obtained. They hurry; they rush; they want to see, and they do see; a quiet murmur runs through the crowd, which weeps with admiration and joy.

Every time a miracle is produced, the same phenomenon recurs. God signals his presence through a subtle shock of the soul that resembles no other shocks here on earth. It is an electric shock that makes you tremble by yourself and cry all at the same time.

God is there! Sublime words that spring from your heart, which is dazzled and overwhelmed. You raise your eyes, and it seems to you that, in the air, a golden swarm of wings is circling around the One who has descended … whom you have come to sense … who at this moment is passing over your heads. 🕊

“ *You raise your eyes.*
God is there! ”

BERNADETTE

CANTICLE

Francis Jammes

La Vierge et les sonnets [the Virgin and the Sonnets], 1919

The Boly mill,
Which has on its pallets
Green mosses
And money that laughs,
Saw the birth of Bernadette.

From this poor mill
Came this child,
Intoxicated with the bread of
    life:
The grains are stripped
In order to make Hosts.

In a village on the slopes of
    the Haute-Pyrénées,
She was nursed
By Marie Arravant
Then returned to her family.

The nurse with the heart of
    gold,
Recalling Bernadette
When she was grown,
Entrusted her with the
    treasure
Of a flock of lambs.

She returned to Lourdes
Around her fifteenth year

In the unfortunate shadow
In which her mother and
    father
Were thrown out of the mill.

She didn't know how to read,
    but
In the evening, the maiden
Spelled out better than in a
    book
The eternal lesson
Above her rosary.

Bernadette was suffering.
She was very little,
Like the Alpine rose
In the forest wind

That trembles, just starting to
    bloom.

But this rose
Attracted the bees
So that the sky brightened,
And it perfumed
The rock of Massabielle.

Close to the rock, this child
—hence the white rose—
Often went to look for
A little bunch of branches.

They were making a fire
At the home of her father and
    mother,

Whose abject poverty
Was lightened a little
Only by this shepherdess.

One day this
Strange news spread
That the Queen of the angels
Was coming from Paradise
To the doorstep of the barns.

And the people were saying:
It is to the shepherdess
Whose name is Bernadette
That the Virgin is appearing
In rocky hideaways.

Shepherds young and old
Speak only in low voices
When, by the Merlasse,
Grave and lowering her eyes,
Bernadette passes by.

As soon as the Pharisees,
Herod with Caiaphas
And the other prelates,
Do not wish to believe in
    anything,
They show their claws.

FIRST APPARITION

Marie-Thérèse Bordenave

La confidente de l'Immaculée [Confident of the Immaculate], 1925

It was February 11, 1858, the second anniversary of the day when Pius IX had declared the work of Le Puy the work of France. It was noon, the hour when the Angelus rang out on all the Pyrenean bell towers. Bernadette, with her sister Toinette[1] and Jeanne Abadie, one of their little neighbors, were going to collect some dry wood on the bank of the Gave, passing through the neighboring meadow of Massabielle. The Savy canal bypassed the rock at that time. The Gave was weak during that period, so that a little bank of sand and pebbles remained dry between the two streams. The waters of the canal itself were not strong, for the mill was not working that day; but we should let Bernadette speak, and we will give here in all its simplicity the account of the first apparition such as we have found it written in her own hand in her personal notes.

The first time I was in the grotto, I was going to collect some wood with two other little girls. When we were at the mill, I asked them if they wanted to go see where the water from the canal joined the Gave. They answered me: Yes. From there we followed the canal, and we found ourselves in front of a grotto. Unable to go any farther, my two companions began to cross the water that was in front of the grotto; so I found myself alone on the other side. I asked the other two if they wanted to help me throw some stones in the water to see if I could pass without taking my shoes off; they told me to do as they had done if I wanted. I went a little farther to see if I could go on without taking my shoes off, but it was useless. Then I went back in front of the grotto. No sooner had I taken off the first stocking than I heard a noise like a gust of wind. I turned my head toward the meadow, I saw the trees

---

1. Who was later named Marie.

"On the bank of the Gave"

were very calm. I continued to take my shoes off; I heard the same sound again, and as I lifted my head, looking at the grotto, I saw a Lady in white. I was a little distressed, and, thinking I was in front of an illusion, I rubbed my eyes, but in vain; I always saw the same Lady. Then I put my hand in my pocket, I took my rosary. Wanting to make the sign of the cross, I wasn't able to get my hand up to my forehead; shock took hold of me even more strongly. The Lady took the rosary that she held between her hands and she made the sign of the cross. I then tried a second time to do it, and I was able to. As soon as I made the sign of the cross, the great shock that I was experiencing disappeared. I knelt down and said the rosary in the presence of this beautiful Lady. After having said the rosary, she motioned to me to come closer, but I didn't dare; then she disappeared.

I began to remove the other stocking in order to cross the little bit of water that was in front of the grotto, and we withdrew.

Along the way, I asked my companions if they had seen anything.—No, they told me, and you, did you see something?—I, Oh! No, if you didn't see anything, I didn't see anything, either. I did not want to tell them; but they begged me so much that I decided to, on

condition that they speak of it to no one. They promised me to keep the secret; but as soon as they arrived home, nothing was more urgent than to tell what I had seen. It was Thursday, February 11, 1858.

Bernadette's account ends here; but history tells us that mother Soubirous, fearing that her daughter was the victim of some illusion, forbade her to return to the grotto. Her motherly solicitude was even more alarmed when she saw Bernadette, seized with strong emotion, begin to cry while reciting evening prayer out loud. She renewed her defense. We went to bed, the child said, but I could not sleep. The very good and gracious figure of the Lady returned constantly to my memory, and I couldn't help remembering what my mother had said to me; I could not believe I had been deceived. 🕊

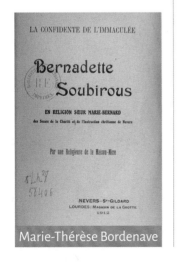

RETURN TO MASSABIELLE

THE OTHER APPARITIONS

Marcelle Auclair

Bernadette, 1958

"We are running to the sweet smell of your perfumes"

At the chime of the bells announcing High Mass, Bernadette and Toinette, under their white capulets, joined the group of schoolgirls who were going to the church.

On leaving, the swarm of girls whose parents let them run in the streets were waiting impatiently for the two sisters.

"Bernadette! Go back to Massabielle! We will go with you!"

"I would like to very much, but I don't dare. My mother says No."

"You're afraid!" said Thérèse.

"If I were in her place, I would be afraid", said Catherine. "If it was the devil!"

"Maybe it is a lost soul!"

"Throw some holy water on it! If your white girl comes on behalf of God, you will see it very well!" said Jeanne Baloum. "Come! If you don't dare ask permission from your mother, I will ask her myself!"

It was nearly eleven o'clock. In front of the church, the Sunday crowd was heading off. Bernadette felt a slight anxiety, but it was on the surface, like a breath of wind that stirs the surface of the water; deep inside herself, there was a great, happy calm. She walked without haste toward the rue des Petits-Fossés, preceded by her sister and Jeanne, who were running, turning around toward her to cry to her:

"Hurry up!"

Jeanne barged into the Soubirous home [located in a former prison] without ceremony:

"Mother Soubirous! Let Bernadette return to the grotto! She will carry holy water with her, and if her white girl is the devil, pfft! Finished!"

"What is she risking? The Abbé himself gave her permission to go there!"

"I do not want it. And if Bernadette fell in the water?"

"There is not enough water there to drown in that place!"

"And if you are not back for Vespers?"

Bernadette took a step forward:

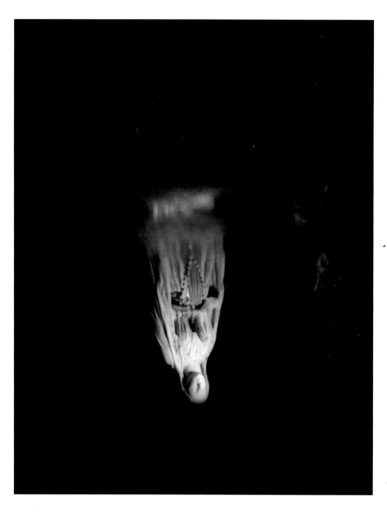

always afraid of learning bad news whenever someone from the house came to check on him at work. One of the most unpleasant was this story of Bernadette at Massabielle.

The less people speak of the poor, the better. The kids in the neighborhood, those from the hospice school, had already made too much noise: twice, when he had passed by close to the fountain, the women had pointed at him and laughed.

He preferred, however, to inform his boss of the rumors that were going around so that he would know well that he, François, a sensible man, had nothing to do with this gossip.

His Bernadette! Usually so rational a girl! To believe that the moon is made of green cheese and to take a white rock for a vision of paradise! For it was undoubtedly only that: a white rock.... So he assumed an arrogant voice to say to Bernadette:

"What's the matter?"

"Mother is giving me permission to go back to Massabielle if you say yes."

"No!" said Soubirous.

Cazenave intervened:

"Let her do it! It is best that she return there in order to understand well that she saw nothing at all."

"And if she sees something?"

"If she sees something, 'that' cannot be bad, since 'that' has a rosary."

Father Soubirous was so upset by this whole affair that he began to cry. It was in order not to appear to reject the advice of his boss that he said to Bernadette:

"I will return on time, I promise you."

Louise knew that her daughter had a habit of keeping her word; but her François had been very upset on Thursday by this story of the little lady. He would surely say no.

And Maï took refuge behind the supreme argument of weak mothers:

"Ask your father for permission."

"He is at the Cazenaves."

"I am coming with you", said Jeanne, who did not want to let go of the heroine of the day.

The other girls were waiting at the door. Bernadette took the lead, followed by her escort. François frowned when he saw his daughter: the poor man had seen so much that he was

"There is a light!

"Go! But I give you only a quarter of an hour."

The little one suddenly felt so relieved, this relief filled her with such resolve that she dared to say:

"A quarter of an hour, that is not enough!"

"Alright. But be back for Vespers, as your mother asked."

Now Bernadette was hurrying.

"Father said yes", she said to Maï as she took from the fireplace an empty bottle for the holy water. Running to fill it at the church font, she was ahead of five of her companions. Other groups were forming, headed by Toinette and Jeanne Baloum. All were poor kids between twelve and fourteen years old, with patched and faded dresses, their naked feet in their clogs.

"I'm afraid!" said Pauline Bourdeau.

"Me, too, I'm afraid", said the others.

Bernadette did not hear them; she was watching the landscape move, she was going so fast, as if something in her were saying to her: "Hurry!"

Her companions were having difficulty following her. When they arrived in front of the grotto, she was already on her knees. They did as she did. Toinette was the last to arrive, and she knelt also.

And they began to say the rosary.

Suddenly Bernadette said:

"There is a light! There it is!"

"Where?"

Bernadette put her arm around the neck of her closest neighbor—a gesture of affection that she often made—and pointed to the grotto:

"Guérat-lo … Qu'at chapelet troussat en bras drect…. Qu'et gaito … (There she is! She has the rosary placed on her right arm…. She is looking at you!)

She laughs! She raises her eyes to heaven…. She greets …

The little lady was in the same place as she was the previous time.

The children saw nothing, but Pauline fled, terrified.

Marie Millot had in her pocket the flask of holy water. She handed it to Bernadette.

"Throw it on her!"

Bernadette went forward and sprinkled the rock with the holy water.

here it is!

"Is she still there?"

"Yes, She is smiling …"

"Go closer!"

Bernadette drew still nearer, and sprinkled again, twice. The "white girl" bowed and smiled.

Jeanne Baloum was above the grotto with some other kids; she saw Bernadette throw the holy water. Furious that she had not waited for her in order to "begin", she cried out:

"Ask her if she comes from God!"

> ## *Bernadette remained motionless,*

"Or from the devil!"

"Go on! Go closer!"

"You are not going closer?"

"Ah! I am going to knock her out, your white girl!"

A stone the size of a one-pound loaf of bread struck against the rock where Bernadette was leaning. It bounced back and fell into the canal with a great splash of water.

The children were terrified and fled like a flock of sparrows, screeching. Bernadette, straight and pale, truly looked like a dead person.

Jeanne and her companions rushed down from the top of the rock. They saw Bernadette, on her knees, motionless.

Two or three girls spoke to her, pushing her, trying to draw her out of that terrifying state in which, with her eyes fixed on the grotto, she seemed to see nothing of what was around her.

"Bad girl!", said Marie to Jeanne, "it was you who threw the stone!"

"Her eyes are wide open", said Justine Soubis, "and yet you'd say she was sleeping."

Jeanne, the guilty one, panicked:

"She looks like an angel, but she is dead!" And everyone began to cry.

"Bernadette! What's the matter with you? Are you sick?"

"Get up! Let's go on!"

Bernadette remained motionless, like a rock.

The strongest ones tried, pulling and pushing, to make her get up, but this slender child seemed to have changed into a granite statue.

The two who were most frightened, who were asking only to flee, left the most courageous ones in the grotto and ran to seek help.

like a rock. ”

On this Sunday when the Savy mill was quiet, as were all mills on all waters, the miller, Jeanne Nicolau, and her sister Jeanne-Marie took advantage of a pale ray of sunshine under the low February sky to walk along the edge of the canal.

The little ones joined the two women:

"Come! Help us! Bernadette Soubirous looks like she's dead on the Massabielle shore."

Running along the path, they recounted the story of the "white girl". Jeanne Nicolau and Jeanne-Marie could see that it seemed impossible to draw Bernadette out of her motionlessness.

No, she was not dead, with her large open eyes, that transparent face, lit from within like a white night light, and that smile, that radiant smile. But what was that?

"I am going to look for my son", said the miller. The miller had a grown son, also a miller, married for two years.

Antoine Nicolau dressed "for Sunday" in order to go to Lourdes, where his comrades were waiting for him at the inn.

He followed his mother, climbing up the forest path, descending by the steep path that goes around the alcove.

They found in the midst of the rocks three or four kids around Bernadette, who was still on her knees, still motionless, still with wide-open eyes, looking at the grotto.

Tears flowed from those eyes; but, crying, she was smiling, and her face was so beautiful that the miller had never seen so beautiful a face. Her hands joined, she was saying the rosary: her lips and her fingers were moving.

He stayed several moment to look at her, seized with admiration and respect, with an emotion in which fear and joy were mixed.

Since a man was there, the girls and women were less afraid, and his admiration and respect won them over.

In the alcove that Bernadette was contemplating, the miller saw nothing.

And he was sorry the smiling child was so pale. But he dared not approach her.

Then his mother said to him:

"Take her, we are going to take her home with us."

He grabbed her arm, but as completely unconscious as she seemed, she resisted the one who wanted to lead her, her eyes remained fixed on what she was looking at there, in the alcove wreathed in brambles.

There was not a whimper, but, after every effort of resistance, she panted for breath. Nicolau ended by lifting her up, holding onto her arm, with his mother holding the other.

When the child was standing, he wiped away the tears that flooded her cheeks, he even put his hand over her eyes to keep her from looking at what she saw and the others did not see. He also tried to bow her head, but she raised it again, her eyes still open, with her same smile.

The two of them, helped by girls who were pushing from behind, had great difficulty in making her climb the trail.

Bernadette was struggling to go back down; it took a lot of strength to lead her.

Antoine Nicolau was a strong man of twenty-nine years; for him, a sack of flour was not heavy, but by himself, he said, it would have taken a lot of work to move Bernadette.

The face of the little Soubirous remained pale; she still had her eyes fixed on high, without seeing anything of what was going on around her.

She really did not seem to hear the questions that the Nicolau mother and her son asked her.

When the group reached the plateau, the miller had worked so hard that, despite the cold, he wiped with the back of his hand the sweat that was soaking his forehead.

It was only on entering the mill, on its very threshold, that Bernadette lowered her eyes and head; and the natural colors returned to her face. The Nicolaus made her sit down in the kitchen. Her companions had timidly followed

her. When she was seated and calm as if nothing had happened, the miller said to her:

"What do you see in that hole? Do you see something that is not pretty?"

"Oh, no! I see a very beautiful young lady! She is all white, she has a rosary on her arm, and she has her hands joined."

Speaking thus, Bernadette pressed her hands against each other, and her face again became as beautiful as at the grotto.

"Stay here, your mother is going to come get you."

And the miller left for Lourdes. On the way, he stopped at the inn that Aunt Bernarde kept, the godmother of the child, and he told her what had happened.

Aunt Bernarde began to moan:

"That little one! My God! What was she thinking, going down there! And what was my sister thinking in letting her go!"

Antoine nodded. And the whole day he could think of nothing else but Bernadette's transfigured face; his heart was heavy—and awestruck.

Toinette had run to tell her mother about it. She found her at the home of Cyprine Gesta, their neighbor.

"Bernadette is at the mill! She saw the white girl! The white girl is following her! She is nearly dead! Come get her!"

"Poor us!" moaned Louise, "me, who had forbidden her to go there! Why did her father let her!"

And Louise waved her right hand.

"I'm telling you she is almost dead!" protested Toinette, who knew that gesture all too well, the prelude to a shower of slaps.

"Dead as dead, she is going to do well! As for you!"

Toinette narrowly avoided the maternal slap, and Mother Soubirous took a stick as thick as her finger, determined to make it the essential argument of her reprimands.

On the way from the mill, Cyprine calmed Maï.

"Leave that stick … Bernadette has surely been very afraid, enough to cure her from going back there … "

Groups were stationed in front of the mill; the rumor had spread that the girl had almost died from having seen the white girl, and they were coming for news.

The miller of Savy left everyone at the door except the mother, the sister, and the neighbor, who entered.

Bernadette was seated near the fire.

She had recovered the ordinary face of a frail and asthmatic little peasant girl, except that she was crying so hard that her apron was soaked with her tears.

Louise Soubirous burst into reproaches:

"How, little rascal, do you make the world run after you?

"But, Maï, I told no one to follow me!"

Louise raised her fist. Cyprine pulled her by the hand, and the miller intervened:

"Don't say anything to her! Take her back to the house, and let her sleep! Your daughter is an angel from heaven!"

But an angel from heaven can cause such disturbances in a poor earthly home that the Soubirous mother collapsed on a chair, crying.

"In any case, I no longer want her to return there! Never again!"

Mother and daughter walked to the house without talking. For Louise, the day's event was like a grave illness that would have imperiled the life of her child: she had had such great fear, in her anger, when Toinette had said to her: "She is almost dead" that the relief of seeing her alive took precedence over everything, for the moment.

But already, concern was reviving.

She looked at her out of the corner of her eye, and, for the first time, the serious expression on her face in repose made an impression on

her, gripped her heart, like the heart of a mother is gripped who detects for the first time in the eyes of her daughter the seriousness of a love.

And what a love! The love of the One who said "I will come like a thief."

Louise, a simple woman, did not understand, and what she did not understand frightened her.

That night, she simply said to François that Bernadette had seen that white thing again, being careful not to arouse his anger; her husband was unhappy enough as it was.

The Soubirous were eating soup with their heads lowered to their bowls, when Basile Casterot interrupted—she who was never seen any more at the home of her sister.

She was red from running and from her outrage:

"Louise! What is this story? Is it decent that people are talking like this about Bernadette?

What happened at Massabielle? What happened at the Savy mill? Child, you would make us sick from the misery that we have in hearing people talk of you! Louise, keep your daughter at home! François, for once in your life, show some authority! All we need after all this noise would be to have you put in prison!"

François lifted his humiliated head.

"I promise you, Basile, that Bernadette will not return to the grotto."

But in Lourdes, already, that Sunday evening, the rumor was growing: "A little poor girl who lives in the dungeon has seen the Virgin at Massabielle!" "The Virgin at Massabielle! We lead the pigs there!" So the gossips were gossiping. And more than one asked: "But who are these Soubirous?"

"*Worse than poor: fallen.*"

There had been many Soubirous in Lourdes, but Bernadette's Soubirous were hated and scorned by brothers, sisters, brothers-in-law, sisters-in-law, and their forty-eight first cousins: the black sheep of the family.

For François and Louise Soubirous were worse than poor: fallen.

Marcelle Auclair

♦ 49

THE MYSTERIOUS LADY REVEALS HER NAME

SIXTEENTH APPEARANCE (Thursday, 25 March)

Jean-Baptiste Estrade

Les Apparitions de Lourdes, 1899

A strong opinion, so strong as to amount to a certainty, prevailed at Lourdes and in all the country round concerning the visions, to the effect that the Lady of the Grotto has not yet said her last word. The wonderful ecstasies, the extraordinary revelation of the spring, the account given by the seer of what was said to her and the messages she carried away all remained without explanation, if She who had appeared continued to keep silence as to her name and the object of her visits. People who had followed the course of events attentively refused to believe that a drama so evidently divine, to judge from its characteristics, could come to an end without leaving behind it anything more than a brilliant but sterile impression. The period from the 4th to the 24th of March had, however, passed away, and no fresh event had taken place to dissipate the clouds of mystery or bring about the expected dénouement.

On this last day, however, the eve of the Annunciation, a breath from heaven stirred many pious souls of the district inspiring them with the desire to go the next day to the Massabielle grotto. As a general rule on the festivals of the Virgin, these good souls were wont to betake themselves for their devotions either to the ancient sanctuary of Garaison or to the no less ancient and venerated sanctuary of Betharram.[1] They hesitated at first as to whether they should follow this inspiration that called them from their traditional place of pilgrimage, from centres of prayer already consecrated, to a spot where the voice of liturgical worship had not yet been heard. The Lady of the rock made the person hesitating understand, as by a secret inspiration, that She who was calling them was one with her whom they invoked at the ancient sanctuaries of the district, and that consequently their homage was directed to the same end.

Text quoted from J. B. Estrade, *The Appearances of the Blessed Virgin Mary at the Grotto of Lourdes: Personal Souvenirs of an Eyewitness*, trans. J. H. Le Breton Girdlestone (Westminster, Eng.: Art & Book, 1912), 120–24.

1. Two places of pilgrimage very popular in the Hautes and Basses Pyrénées. One is situated in the eastern portion of the diocese of Tarbes, whilst the other on the west is in the diocese of Bayonne.

Instantly their scruples were appeased and the pilgrims directed their steps to Lourdes.

There were not, however, at the grotto on that day the enormous crowds of the previous days. Several men were kneeling here and there, but it was chiefly young virgins and pious matrons who formed the hidden Lady's guard of honor. In obeying the interior impulse of which they had been conscious, all these holy souls had been penetrated by the thought that some great event was about to take place at the grotto. They wondered beforehand what that event could be. Was the mysterious Lady going to raise the veil which hid her and show herself, as they had hoped she would do on March 4, in all the splendor of her glory and the majesty of her heavenly perfections? Would she accomplish, by means of the new pool of Siloam, one of those wonders of healing which restore strength and joy to suffering hearts? Would she take the opportunity offered by the festival of the day itself, suggested, it would seem, by the very title of the Annunciation, to declare her name and reveal her heavenly origin? All these hypotheses presented themselves to the minds of the pilgrims and were the object of a thousand prayers and hopes.

That inward voice which the friends of the Virgin had heard had also spoken, but with more intimate affection, to the heart of Bernadette. That voice was no strange voice to the child; it was the faithful messenger that always announced the coming visit of the Lady of grace and love.

During the happy days after the fortnight of the Appearances the little seer had often knelt beneath the holy rock. In obedience to the desires of her soul she often raised her eyes to the beloved recess, but alas! It ever remained empty and no heavenly light came to lighten it. One may judge of Bernadette's joy at knowing that the Mother called her to yet another meeting. Little did the child trouble herself about the anticipations of the people as to what the Lady might or might not do. Her own faith was firmly rooted, and her one and only desire was to gaze once more upon the charms of that august Sovereign who summed up in her own person all the graces and beauties of heaven.

In the family circle, on the evening of March 24, Bernadette told her parents of the interior monition she had received and spoke as of a certainty of the happiness that awaited her next day at the grotto. Full of this thought she went to bed, but sleep refused to come to her. The night seemed long and many an *Ave Maria* fell from her lips. As soon as the earliest lights of day appeared she left her bed, dressed quickly, and without troubling about the asthma from which she was then suffering, hastened along the road to Massabielle, and covered she was indeed with shame and confusion at finding the recess already aglow with glory and the Lady waiting.

"She was there," said Bernadette, "peaceful, smiling and looking down upon the crowd like a loving mother looking at her children."

"When I was on my knees before the Lady," she continued, "I asked her pardon for arriving late. Always good and gracious, she made a

sign to me with her head to tell me that I need not excuse myself. Then I spoke to her of all my affection, all my respect and the happiness I had in seeing her again. After having poured out my heart to her I took up my rosary. While I was praying, the thought of asking her name came before my mind with such persistence that I could think of nothing else. I feared to be presumptuous in repeating a question she had always refused to answer and yet something compelled me to speak. At last, under an irresistible impulsion, the words fell from my mouth, and I begged the Lady to tell me who she was.[2] The Lady did as she had always done before; she bowed her head and smiled but she did not reply. I cannot say why, but I felt myself bolder and asked her again to graciously tell me her name; however she only bowed and smiled as before, still remaining silent. Then once more, for the third time, clasping my hands and confessing myself unworthy of the favor I was asking of her, I again made my request."

When the child reached this point in her story she was overcome by emotion. She continued as follows.

"The Lady was standing above the rose-tree, in a position very similar to that shown in the Miraculous Medal. At my third request her face became very serious and she seemed to bow down in an attitude of humility. Then she joined her hands and raised them to her breast … she looked up to heaven … then slowly opening her hands and leaning forward toward me, she said to me in a voice vibrating with emotion,

"'I AM THE IMMACULATE CONCEPTION.'"[3]

In pronouncing these last words, Bernadette lowered her head and reproduced the Lady's gesture.

The great mystery of the grotto was at length revealed! And on what a day—on the anniversary of that thrice blessed day when the archangel Gabriel came from the Most High to announce the impending advent of the Redeemer so long expected, and to salute as "full of grace", *i.e., Immaculate*, the predestined woman who was to crush the head of the accursed serpent. What a ground of hope for us, this coincidence. Angels who surrounded the Virgin in her rustic shrine, what must have been your joy on hearing your august Sovereign describe herself by one of the most glorious of her glorious titles. The vaults of Massabielle must have resounded with your hymns of praise.

The pilgrims kneeling at the grotto heard nothing but they were conscious of intense happiness within their souls. During the ecstasy they hung upon any words from the seer's lips, hoping every instant that some words of revelation would fall from her innocent mouth. When Bernadette had finished speaking an unutterable emotion seized all there present and they fell upon their knees. After having offered this first act

Jean-Baptiste Estrade

The Lady.

2. Bernadette did not say in what words she had made her request.

3. In patois, *Qué soy er' Immaculata Counception*.

of homage to the Lady, in transports of enthusiasm they went, some to place their lips against the holy rock, others to take in their arms as a living being or a holy relic the branches of the rose-tree hanging down from the recess. From the midst of the crowd, from the little islets in the Gave, from the top of the hill, there rose the popular invocation, *O Mary, conceived without sin, pray for us who have recourse to you.*

Very shortly after the Appearance, the town of Lourdes was full of the young seer's great news. The inhabitants shook hands on meeting in the street, congratulating one another as on a happy event which had befallen them. As to the strangers, they could not tear themselves away from the grotto; after having said one decade they said another and when they had finished singing they began again. At length, when night fell, they dispersed in various directions, proclaiming wherever they passed the Virgin's words.[4]

LITANIES OF BERNADETTE

Paul Claudel

April 22, 1937

Saint Bernadette,
Pray, pray for us!

Serene shepherdess,
Pray, pray for us!

Lady shepherdess,
Pray, pray for us!

Little daisy,
Pray, pray for us!

Child with the sweet heart,
Pray, pray for us!

Drop of water from the
Gave,
Pray, pray for us!

Fearless and pure eye,
Pray, pray for us!

Maid of the Azure,
Pray, pray for us!

Finder of resources,
Pray, pray for us!

Opener of a spring,
Pray, pray for us!

Since God chose you,
Pray, pray for us!

In order to contemplate
Mary,
Pray, pray for us!

After so much suffering,
Pray, pray for us!

And so much patience,
Pray, pray for us!

Perfect in poverty,
Pray, pray for us!

In steadiness,
Pray, pray for us!

In order to contemplate
always,
Pray, pray for us!

The Mother of Love,
Pray, pray for us!

We say on our knees:
Pray, pray for us!

Bernadette Soubirous,
Pray, pray for us!

Paul Claudel

"*Serene shepherdess,
Pray, pray for us!*"

L'AN DE GRACE 1858
DANS LE CREUX DU ROCHER OU L'ON VOIT
SA STATUE, LA SAINTE VIERGE APPARUT
A BERNADETTE 18 FOIS ; LE 11 ET LE 14
FÉVRIER ; CHAQUE JOUR, DEUX EXCEPTÉS,
DU 18 FÉVRIER AU 4 MARS ; LE 25 MARS ;
LE 7 AVRIL ; LE 16 JUILLET.

LA SAINTE VIERGE DIT A L'ENFANT,
LE 18 FÉVRIER : « VOULEZ-VOUS ME FAIRE
« LA GRACE DE VENIR ICI PENDANT QUINZE
« JOURS ? – JE NE VOUS PROMETS PAS DE
« VOUS RENDRE HEUREUSE DANS CE MONDE
« MAIS DANS L'AUTRE. – JE DÉSIRE QU'IL
« VIENNE DU MONDE. »

LA VIERGE LUI DIT PENDANT LA QUIN-
ZAINE : « VOUS PRIEREZ POUR LES PÉ-
« CHEURS. VOUS BAISEREZ LA TERRE POUR
« LES PÉCHEURS. – PÉNITENCE, PÉNITENCE,
« PÉNITENCE. – ALLEZ DIRE AUX PRÊTRES
« DE FAIRE BÂTIR ICI UNE CHAPELLE. :
« JE VEUX QU'ON Y VIENNE EN PROCESSION.
« ALLEZ BOIRE A LA FONTAINE ET VOUS
« Y LAVER. ALLEZ MANGER DE CETTE
« HERBE QUI EST LÀ

LE 25 MARS LA VIERGE DIT :
JE SUIS L'IMMACULÉE CONCEPTION.

CANONIZATION OF BERNADETTE

Pope Pius XI

December 8, 1933

HOMILY

Pronounced on the occasion of the canonization of Blessed Bernadette Soubirous (December 8, 1933).

We are deeply delighted to have been granted once again during the course of this Holy Year the opportunity to gather new flowers of holiness in the garden of the Church and to offer them, all fragrant with heavenly sweetness, to the admiration of the Catholic universe.

This same child from Lourdes to whom We awarded the palm of the blessed a few years ago has been distinguished by new and marvelous miracles that have been recognized as authentic after the examinations prescribed by law; this is why We have decided, with very great joy, to accord her new and solemn honors.

It is, besides, impossible not to see the secret design of the divinity in this event.

The present year, which We have dedicated especially to the memory of the redemption of man, in facts ends the fifteenth lustrum since the Virgin Mother of God, immaculate in her conception, showed herself to this very innocent young girl, near the rock of Massabielle. It seems, therefore, that God, sovereign Master of time and events, wanted to increase the splendor of this jubilee still more. For all that is done in praise of Bernadette Soubirous redounds as glory for the Immaculate Conception. The Immaculate One has, in fact, loved Bernadette in so maternal a way that she has entrusted to this very humble shepherdess the order to publish her privileges and to call men to repentance.

"God", says the apostle, "chose what is foolish in the world to shame the wise. God chose what is weak in the world to shame the strong." His very holy Mother does the same.

It is worth noting, in fact, that the Blessed Virgin Mary, wishing to illustrate in a miraculous way that the pontifical sentence by which Our predecessor Pius IX of happy memory had proclaimed on this very day and in this very basilica, the dogma of the Immaculate Conception to the applause of the whole universe, was addressed, not to men of high science, but to a simple miller's ignorant daughter, who possessed no other wealth than the sole candor of her exquisite soul, and it was to this girl that she said: "I am the Immaculate

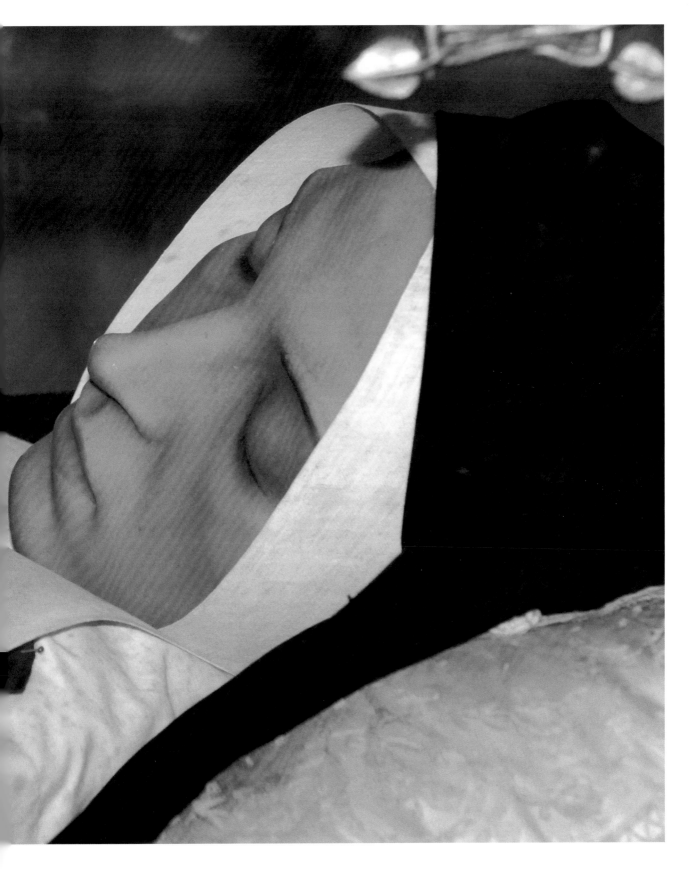

Conception." Likewise, in her plan to awaken the Catholic faith in the hearts of men and to bring their corrupt morals back to the right path of Christian virtue, she did not turn to the rich and the powerful of this world or to the leaders of people. She preferred to them the one who could say: "Blessed are the poor in spirit, for the Kingdom of heaven is theirs. Blessed are the pure of heart, for they will see God." Also, under the guidance of the Queen of Heaven and thanks to the docile assistance of her servant, three sanctuaries were erected near the rock of Massabielle, and the faithful of all nations flock there, either as a group or individually, in order to beg for divine assistance. A grand spectacle, venerable Brothers and dear Sons, that commands universal admiration, not excepting those who lack the light of the Catholic faith! Lourdes! Admire in Lourdes the honor and glory of the immaculate Virgin Mary. But see at the same time a unique monument to the authentic holiness of Marie-Bernadette Soubirous. How many men who had strayed off the path of Christian truth have returned, thanks to Lourdes, to the bosom of their mother the Church! How many others, soiled with the mire of vices, have been led by Lourdes to a better life! How many others still have sensed there the divine invitation and have entered resolutely into the ways of perfection! Finally, how many infirm and sick have found again there, through divine virtue, the fullness of strength and health!

We ourselves, at this time when we are canonizing this child of Lourdes, experience the need to go in spirit and heart to this Grotto of the Immaculate Virgin in order to render our homage. We, too, feel the need to pray with you to this Mother of heaven on this day that is dedicated to her so that we might never cease to walk in the very holy footsteps of Bernadette Soubirous, whose virtues and illustrious examples are proposed today for our imitation. Let us strive to reproduce her modesty and her humility, her faith and her ardent charity; and just as she constantly responded

to the heavenly inspirations with a perfect fidelity, we, too, must be able to respond with a good heart to the grace of God who calls us to a holier and more perfect state. So that even if it is not possible for us to equal her in innocence of life, let us try at least to have the same zeal for penance, each according to his condition.

We have, in addition to this, the strong desire that ardent prayers be addressed to the Immaculate Mother of God and to her servant for the whole Catholic universe, so that all might receive, during the Holy Year, the goods of the divine Redemption that Christ our Lord won for us through his blood and so that all might also obtain that peace which the world cannot give, which consists in the tranquility of order and that is acquired through the faithful fulfillment of Christian precepts.

Please God—We ask him through the intercession of the Immaculate Virgin Mary and of his very faithful servant Bernadette Soubirous—that "we might always experience within ourselves the fruits of his Redemption, through Christ our Lord".

Amen. 🕊

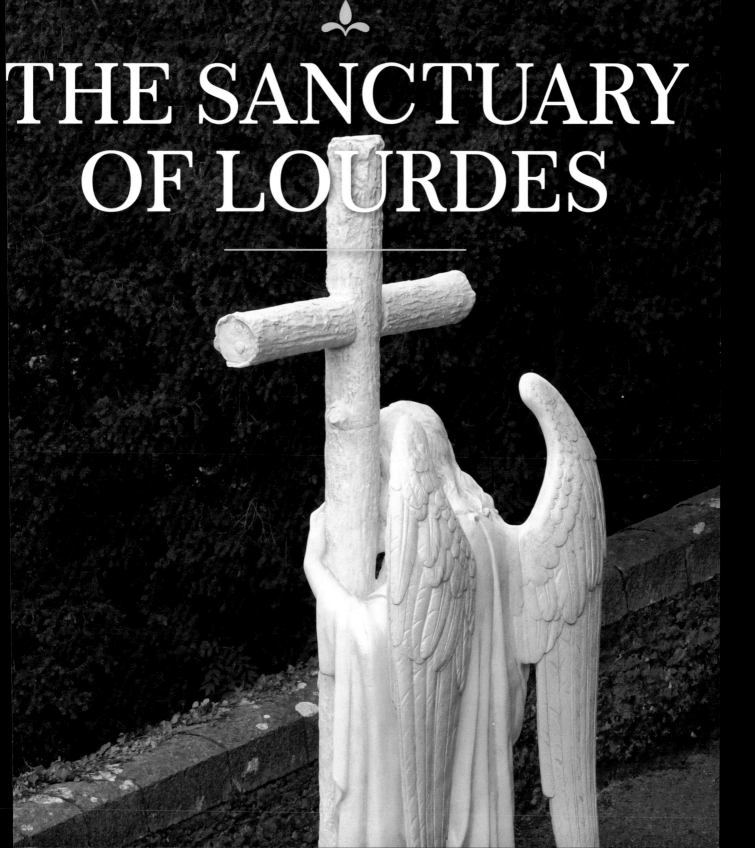

THE SANCTUARY
OF LOURDES

STATUE OF THE VIRGIN

Henri Lasserre

Notre-Dame de Lourdes, 1892

Notwithstanding the bishop's pastoral letter [which recognized the truth of the divine events at the Grotto], the Church had not yet taken possession by any public ceremony of these forever sacred places. This, however, was solemnly done April 4, 1864, by the inauguration and benediction of a superb statue of the Blessed Virgin, which was placed, with all the pomp usual on such occasions, in the rustic niche wreathed with wild roses, where the Mother of God had made her appearance to the daughter of man.

> ## "The grand fête of earth and heaven."

The weather was magnificent. The sun of early spring had risen and was progressing through the azure dome of heaven, which was not specked with a single cloud.

The town of Lourdes was dressed with flowers, banners, garlands, and triumphal arches. From the high tower of the parish church, from all the chapels of the town, and from all the churches of the neighborhood, joyous peals of bells burst forth. Vast multitudes had assembled to take part in this grand *fête* of earth and heaven. A procession such as never had been seen within the memory of man, started in order to proceed from the parish church of Lourdes to the Grotto of the Apparition. Bodies of troops, in all the splendor of military equipment, led the way. Immediately following them were the Brotherhoods of Lourdes; the mutual-aid societies; all the corporations of the adjoining districts, bearing their banners and cross; the Congregation of the Children of Mary, whose flowing robes shone like snow; the Sisters of Nevers with their long black veils; the Sisters of Charity, in large white caps; the Sisters of Saint Joseph, enveloped in their dark cloaks; the religious orders of men, Carmelites and teaching Brothers of the

Text quoted from Henri Lasserre, *Our Lady of Lourdes*, 11th ed. (New York: P. J. Kenedy and Sons, 1906), 482–86.

Christian Schools, immense multitudes of pilgrims, men, women and children, not forgetting old men, in all, fifty to sixty thousand human beings, ranged in two interminable files, wound along the road, strewn with flowers, leading to the illustrious Rocks of Massabielle. At intervals, choruses of human voices and bands of instrumental music made the air resound with triumphal marches, canticles, and all the outbursts of popular enthusiasm. Lastly, bringing up the rear of this unheard-of procession, the most eminent prelate, Monseigneur Bertrand-Sévère Laurence, Bishop of Tarbes, surrounded by four hundred priests in full canonicals, by his grand vicars, and by the dignitaries of the chapter of his cathedral church, marched with solemn steps, wearing his mitre and attired in his pontifical robes, blessing with one hand the assembled people, while with the other he supported himself on his large golden crozier.

An indescribable emotion, a kind of intoxication such as is known only by Christian multitudes assembled in the sight of God, filled all hearts. In fact, the day of solemn triumph had come, after so many difficulties, so many struggles, so many obstacles. Tears of happiness, enthusiasm, and love trickled down the cheeks of these masses of people, agitated by the breath of God.

What ineffable joy must, in the midst of this fête, have filled the heart of Bernadette, who, doubtless, marched at the head of the Congregation of the Children of Mary! What feelings of overwhelming felicity must have inundated the soul of the venerable Curé of Lourdes, as he chanted, without doubt, at the bishop's side, the Hosanna of the Divine victory? Both of them having been partakers of the affliction, the moment was now come for both of them to be present at the glory.

Alas! Bernadette was sought for in vain among the Children of Mary; the Curé Peyramale was sought for in vain among the clergy who surrounded the Prelate. There are joys too great for earth and which are reserved for heaven. Here below, God refuses them even to his dearest sons.

At the very time when everything wore a festal air and the sun shone joyously on the triumph of the faithful, the Curé of Lourdes, attacked with a malady which was pronounced mortal, was the victim of the most terrible physical sufferings. He was lying stretched on his bed of pain, at the foot of which two religieuses connected with the hospital, prayed and watched day and night. He wished to have been lifted from his bed to have seen the grand cortege, but his strength failed him, and he had not even a passing glimpse of all its splendor. Through the closed curtains of his apartment, the joyous sound of the silvery bells only reached him like a funeral knell.

As to Bernadette, God marked His predilection for her as is His wont to do with His elect by causing her to pass through the grand trial of pain. While, presiding over the immense procession of the faithful, Monseigneur Laurence, Bishop of Tarbes, was going in the name of the Church to take possession of the Rocks of Massabielle and solemnly inaugurate the veneration of the Virgin who had appeared to her, Bernadette, like the eminent Priest of whom we have just spoken, was brought low by sickness; and maternal Providence, fearing

Henri Lasserre

perhaps for her much-loved child the temptation of vainglory, deprived her of the sight of
those unheard-of fêtes, where she would have
heard her own name re-echoed with acclama-
tion by thousands of voices, and celebrated
from the Christian pulpit by the ardent words
of those who preached on the occasion. Too
poor to receive proper attention at home, where

neither she nor any of her family had ever
wished to receive any pecuniary aid, Bernadette
had been carried to the hospital where she lay
on the humble pallet of public charity, in the
midst of poor creatures, whom this transitory
world terms wretched, but whom Jesus Christ
has blessed, by declaring them the inheritors of
His eternal kingdom.

THE SANCTUARY EMERGES

Henri Lasserre

Notre-Dame de Lourdes, 1892

Let us return to Lourdes.

Time had proceeded on its course. Human hands had set to work in good earnest.

The approaches to the Grotto, in which the Virgin had appeared, were changed in appearance. Without losing aught of its grandeur, this wild and stern locality had assumed a graceful, pleasing, and lively aspect. A superb church not yet finished, but swarming with workmen proudly seated on the summit of the rocks of Massabielle, towered joyously towards heaven. The great slope, abrupt and uncultivated, formerly accessible only with difficulty even to the practiced feet of mountaineers, was covered with green turf and planted with shrubs and flowers. Amidst dahlias and roses, daisies and violets, beneath the shade of acacias and laburnum, a vast path, broad as a road, wound in graceful curves and led from the church to the Grotto [tracing on the ground the shape of an M., the initial of Mary's name].

The Grotto was closed with an iron railing, after the fashion of a sanctuary. A golden lamp was suspended from the roof. Under those wild rocks on which the Virgin had trodden with her divine feet, clusters of tapers burned night and day.

Outside this enclosed portion, the miraculous spring fed four massive basins of bronze. A piscina, concealed from observation by a small building erected over it, afforded the sick an opportunity of bathing in the blessed water.

The situation of the millstream of Savy had been altered, being thrown back up the stream in the direction of the Gave. The Gave itself had retreated to afford room for a magnificent road which led to these Rocks of Massabielle, formerly so totally unknown, but now so celebrated. On the banks of the river as it flowed downwards, the soil had been levelled, and a broad lawn bordered with elms and poplars formed a splendid promenade.

> ## *Of an M which means Mary!*

Text quoted from Henri Lasserre, *Our Lady of Lourdes*, 11th ed. (New York: P. J. Kenedy and Sons, 1906), 477–79.

All these changes had been effected and were still being effected in the midst of an immense influx of believers. The copper coins thrown into the Grotto by the faith of the people, the grateful ex-votos of so many invalids who had been cured, of so many hearts that had been consoled, of so many souls that had been restored as it were from death to truth and life, sufficed to defray the expenses of these gigantic labors, the estimate of which was nearly two million francs. When God in his goodness condescends to call on man to cooperate directly in any one of his works, he employs neither soldiers nor gendarmes to collect the sums needful, and only accepts a purely voluntary assistance from the hands of his creatures. The Master of the world repudiates constraint, for He is the God of free souls, and the only tributes He consents to receive are the spontaneous gifts offered to him from a happy heart and entire independence by those by whom He is loved.

Thus was the church being built; thus was the millstream and the river diverted into other courses; thus were the adjoining lands excavated or levelled, and roads laid around the celebrated Rocks where the Mother of Christ had manifested herself in her glory to the gaze of mortals.

" *May the blessings touch the heart of Mary Immaculate* "

CONSECRATION OF THE BASILICA OF THE IMMACULATE CONCEPTION

A Cleric

1876

On July 1st, toward five o'clock in the evening, the episcopal procession went to the crypt. The bishop of Tarbes was waiting for it there. When Cardinal Guibert crossed the threshold of the Sanctuary, Bishop Jourdan spoke:

"Eminence", he said, "the bishop, the clergy and the faithful of the diocese of Tarbes are happy to receive you and to greet in your person the delegate and representative of the august Pius IX. May the blessings that Your Eminence brings us from so high, joined to those of His Excellency the Apostolic Nuncio and of our Lords the Archbishops and Bishops here present touch the heart of Mary Immaculate and obtain the triumph of our Holy Mother the Church and the salvation of France!"

Bishop Guibert expressed his thanks in emotional terms and showed what precious favors were tied to the solemnity of the consecration.

The procession entered the crypt. The already numerous crowd of pilgrims walked behind it, eager to witness the Deposition of the Holy Relics. This touching ceremony was carried out under the direction of Bishop Cataldi. His Eminence Cardinal Guibert and, after him, each of the fifteen archbishops and bishops appointed for the consecration of the altars of the Basilica, acknowledged the Relics, declared them authentic, and sealed them with their seal. When these solemn recognitions were over, the Relics remained exposed in the chapel of the Sacred Heart for the veneration of the faithful.

The next day, Sunday, July 2, at eight o'clock in the morning, the large procession set off to the sound of the bells. Having left the episcopal house, it walked toward the Basilica. Four priests in red chasubles

carried honorary stretchers destined to receive the Relics.

After the singing of the Penitential Psalms before the Holy Relics, and after that of the Litanies before the door of the Basilica, the cardinal proceeded to the triple sprinkling of the outer walls of the church. Then he performed inside the chapel the various rites prescribed by the liturgy.

The episcopal procession left the Basilica and went again to the crypt, and soon the Holy Relics appeared that had been carried in procession around the church. When the procession made its entrance into the holy place, the

faithful were allowed to come into the temple. Those who were fortunate enough to have been able to find a place there contemplated with delight the most moving ceremonies.

The bishops of Aix, Auch, Perga, Chambéry, Reims, Albi, Vannes, Digne, Annecy, Marseille, Nantes, Montauban, Grenoble, Toulouse, and Nevers were the fifteen who were to assist His Eminence in the consecration of the altars. Each of these prelates presented himself before the cardinal, received from him, on a veil of red silk, the Relics destined for the altar that he was to consecrate, and stood in a semi-circle around the main altar. At a signal given by the master of ceremonies, all the bishop-

" *The people venerated the Relics in silence.* "

consecrators raised their hands and showed the reliquary. The most profound recollection reigned in the large audience, and the Christian people venerated the Relics in silence.

These precious remains of the holy bodies were deposited in the sepulcher of the altar of which it was to be the richest treasure and the most beautiful ornament. It is, in fact, on these blessed bones that the mystic Lamb wishes to renew his immolation and perpetuate the fruits of his sacrifice.

While Cardinal Guibert was doing the anointings and other ceremonies required by the Pontifical at the altar of the Immaculate

metropolitan of the province of Auch. After the Gospel, the illustrious and eloquent bishop of Hébron gave a magnificent discourse, in which he showed that the solemnity of this day is the dazzling affirmation of Christianity considered either in its integral doctrine or in its social influence. Bishop Mermillod said in conclusion that the Basilica of Lourdes is a monument raised to affirm that the world can be saved only through the supernatural of the Gospel, penetrating minds with its doctrine and the living forces of modern societies with its action. And his moving words greeted the future of France, become once again the nation of Christ.

After Mass, His Eminence Cardinal Guibert give the papal benediction to which is attached a plenary indulgence. 🕊

Conception, the consecrator-bishops were reproducing them at their respective altars.

The faithful again saw with great emotion the anointing of the church walls. The holy chrism flowed over the stone and marked the sign of salvation on it twelve times. The choir then sang of the riches and splendors of the House of God:

"There is Jerusalem, that great city of the heavens, adorned like the Bride of the Lamb, because she has become his tabernacle.... Your walls, O Jerusalem, are made of precious stones.... Your squares will be covered with the purest gold. Alleluia! You will shine with a brilliant light, all the nations of the earth will adore you, and in all your streets voices will join together to repeat Alleluia! Alleluia!"

The Basilica was consecrated. The pontifical Mass was celebrated by Msgr. De Langalarie,

. . . AND CROWNING OF OUR LADY OF LOURDES

A Cleric

1876

The next day, July 3, 1876, at nine-thirty in the morning, the bells of the Basilica rang and announced the beginning of the ceremony that was the object of all wishes. An immense crowd covered the esplanade and Savy meadow. A magnificent spectacle was offered here to angels and men. Having left the episcopal house as on the day before, the procession unfolded its majestic and sparkling rings in the midst of eager waves of pilgrims whose numbers were ever increasing. The vast enclosure prepared in the plain had become insufficient.

Some gathered on the terrace that extended to the east of the Basilica; others spread out over the large ramp that is at its feet; others attached themselves to the slopes of the Calvary mountain and formed, by superimposing themselves according to the features of the terrain, gigantic human clusters. The trees that bordered the Gave were not spared in this invasion of pious as well as daring curiosity. We see emerging from the fold of their branches the fresh, joyous faces of the children of the valley, they, too, eager with the emotions of so beautiful a feast and wanting to celebrate the new glory of the Good Mother.

When the episcopal procession arrived, not without effort, at the platform erected on the esplanade of the Rosary, Bishop Meglia celebrated pontifically the holy mysteries. But the sacred hymns were interrupted. A great voice was heard. The bishop of Poitiers gave a wonderful homily that delighted the immense audience and would remain in the annals of the Christian pulpit as one of the most beautiful memorials raised to the glory of Our Lady of Lourdes.

With the twofold authority of an irresistible logic and an eloquence full of charm in its most vigorous tones, the eminent orator reduced to nothing the vain

> "*Queen of Heaven*"

objections of incredulity and caused, in the full light of theological certitude, the truth of the Apparition of the Immaculate at the Grotto to shine out. At the end of Mass, the apostolic nuncio gave the blessing in the name of the pope. And the crowd prostrated itself, happy to bow down a second time under the hand of a delegate of Pius IX.

Bishop Meglia then intoned the *Ave Maris Stella*. All the audience continued singing the hymn so dear to Catholic hearts. At the same time, the representative of the Sovereign Pontiff climbed the steps that led to the throne on which was placed a beautiful statue of Mary Immaculate. He carried in his hands the diadem of gold and diamonds.... In the midst of an immense gathering, in sight of a hundred thousand persons, the nuncio placed the crown on the radiant forehead of the Blessed Virgin....

Great applause resounded at this solemn moment. The multitude was overcome by the liveliest emotion; the tears of pious affection wet the eyelids; all mouths were united in glorifying the Immaculate Mother ... Long live Our Lady of Lourdes! Long live Our Lady of Lourdes! Long live Pius IX! Long live Our Lady of Lourdes! Such were the cheers that resounded; such were the cries of love and hope that escaped from all hearts: Long live Pius IX! Long live Our Lady of Lourdes! But the nuncio sang: Regina Caeli Laetare, Alleluia! A formidable choir repeated these joyous congratulations. With these tones, the enthusiasm of the crowd redoubled: Alleluia! Alleluia! The thousands of voices repeated, and the cheers began again: Long live Our Lady of Lourdes! Long live Our Lady of Lourdes!

Then silence fell. On the chair placed in front of the great platform, a new speaker appeared.

It was a bishop; it was the bishop of Tarbes. It was understood that he was coming to interpret the feelings that were filling all hearts. His words, in fact, were a tribute inspired by gratitude. It was offered to Pius IX first of all: to Pius IX, the Pontiff of the Immaculate Conception, whose kind and beautiful image, reproduced in mosaic on the pediment of the Basilica, presided over so beautiful a solemnity and whose venerated name would also live in the memory of the pilgrims at Lourdes.

The prelate, who was speaking, one sensed, the language of the heart, then addressed the expression of his gratitude to the cardinal, to the nuncio, and to the bishops who enhanced the splendor of the Lourdes festivals by the radiance of their presence. The illustrious speakers heard in the various ceremonies of these beautiful days were not forgotten. They received from Bishop Jourdan gratitude that was felt all the more because it was translated into the most delicate praise.

The procession formed once again and was directed toward the Basilica, where Bishop Meglia placed a second crown on the statue that dominated the main altar. It soon left the sacred precinct and was taken to the episcopal house. The bishops took their place on a lawn, elevated in the form of a terrace to the north of the building. The crowd knelt and received with joy the solemn blessing of all the prelates....

May the Queen of Heaven, glorified at Lourdes with so much brilliance, always smile on her children on earth! May their supplications touch her heart! May she grant them the joy of seeing the triumph of the Church and the Christian regeneration of France!

THE NEW LOURDES

Bernard Dauberive

The Pilgrim and Tourist Guide, 1896

After crossing the Gave on the bridge of the boulevard built in 1881, one's gaze embraces the Esplanade, an immense park that leads directly to the Church of the Rosary, to the Basilica, and to the Grotto. Note in the midst of mounds of greenery a bronze Saint Michael and the Breton cross. Farther on, in the old Savy meadow, the crowned statue of the Mother of God (the work of M. Raffl); on the right, the Pilgrim Shelter, a vast building that encloses an immense room filled with benches; on the left, the magnificent printshop of the Rev. Fathers (Imprimerie des RR. Pères).

To reach the Grotto, you pass the Rosary on the right and go along the Gave. The entrance to the cave is protected by a grate. The white marble statue of the Virgin (by M. Fabisch) stands majestically at the bottom. Around its head, you can read the inscription in enameled letters: "I am the Immaculate Conception." Crutches line the walls, and more than two hundred candles burn continually on the large iron harrows, large ones costing fifty francs and small ones twenty-five francs. On the right is a marble chair, benches, and chairs.

During the pilgrimages, you can see a magnificent rolling altar, covered with engraved silver plaques.

On the left of the Grotto is the miraculous fountain whose water falls through three faucets into a basin. One part flows through twelve faucets for the use of the pilgrims; the other feeds the swimming pools. The source provides over thirteen

hundred gallons an hour, thirty-two thousand gallons per day.

About a hundred feet from the fountain are the swimming pools, built in 1892. They consist of three rooms: one for men, one for ladies, one for children. The water is renewed only three times a day, around 11 o'clock, 3 o'clock, and from 7 to 9 o'clock in the evening. In the morning, until 6 o'clock, and in the evening from 7 to 9 p.m., people in good health are admitted to them. All the rest of the time, they are reserved for the use of the infirm.

To the west of the Grotto stretch the Lacets, well-used paths on the hill that place it in communication with the Basilica.

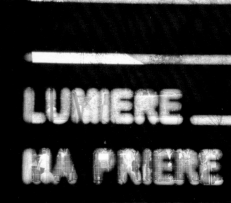

With money coming from all parts of the Christian world, the magnificent chapel requested by the Queen of Heaven was built. It consists of three parts: the Basilica, the Crypt, and the Church of the Rosary.

The Basilica, a masterpiece of grace and lightness in the style of the thirteenth century, rises triumphantly to the summit of the Massabielle rocks. It was placed just above the Grotto and consists of two parts: the upper church and the Crypt. It was built under the episcopate of Bishop Laurence by M. Hippolyte Durand, the diocesan architect. The exterior of the monument is in Lourdes stone; the interior, in the white stone of Angoulême.

The spire, of wonderful workmanship, wears at its summit a crown of gold. A chime repeats every quarter of an hour the first phrase of the "Parce Domine" antiphon

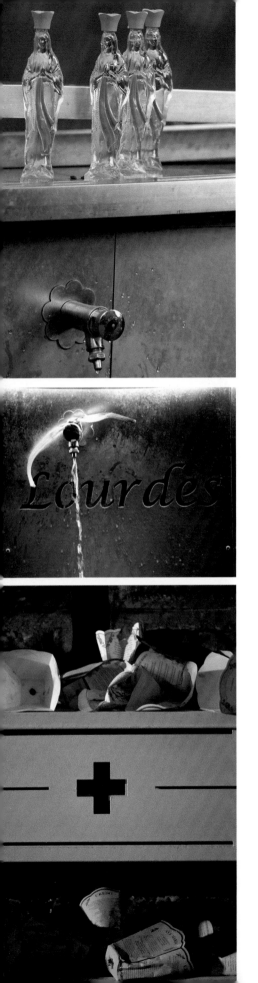

in response to the words of the Mother of God: "Penance! Penance! Penance!"

The bells, forged in Paris in M. Hildebrand's workshops, were offered in 1873 to Our Lady of Lourdes by Prince Gastonde Béarn. The first, Jeanne-Alphonsine (weight: 4,409 lbs.) had Alphonse XII of Bourbon and Mlle. Jeanne-Marie de Béarn as sponsors. The second, Geneviève-Félicie (weight: 968 lbs.), sponsored by Archbishop Pierre-Félix of Tours and Mme. the Duchess of Vallombreuse. The third, Hermine-Benoite (weight: 2,425 lbs.), sponsored by Bishop Langénieux of Tarbes and Mme. the Princess of Léon. The fourth, Cécile-Gastine (weight: 1,764 lbs.), sponsored by the Prince and Princess of Béarn.

Above the large rose window, admire the mosaic that came from the Vatican workshops. It represents Pope Pius IX. The length of the building is 167 feet, its width is 69 feet.

At the entrance, the statue of the Virgin in white marble.

To the right and left, the Immaculate Conception and Saint Bernard. Over the tympanum of the door, Jesus blessing the pilgrims.

As soon as the visitor has looked into the nave, he can only be filled with admiration: silk and gold are everywhere. Testimonials of thanksgiving line the church from top to bottom. Immense banners coming from all the countries of the world hang from the vault of the sanctuary.

Among the most beautiful, we note: Metz (the Virgin surrounded by a lily), Brittany (the Sacred Heart within glory), Our Lady of Africa (the Black Virgin), Our Lady of Fourvière (the arms of the city of Lyon).

A gold grate surrounds the choir.

The high altar, all in marble from Carrare, is the work of two men from Lyon, MM. Bresson and Bonnet. Five bas-reliefs adorn the lower part. They represent the Visitation, the Annunciation, the Assumption, the Crowning, and the Apparition in the Grotto. On feast days, an immense carpet, designed in Blois and embroidered by the Dames de France, covers the mosaics of the church.

The altar is dominated by the statue of the Virgin (by M. Cabuchet). The crown consists of twelve golden stars with diamonds. Below the statue has been placed the golden palm decorated with enamels, given by Pius IX. The following inscription is read there: "From pious souls of Majorca to Pius I, martyr and confessor."

There are twenty chandeliers arranged in a circle around the tabernacle and twelve lamps, the most beautiful of which are those from Ireland, Valencia, and Macao (China).

Note on the sides of the sanctuary the ex-votos, the crosses of honor, officers' epaulettes, swords, ships, the golden Rosary of Poitiers, flags from England, Belgium, Hungary, etc.; the windows of the nave that picture the principal figures of the Old and New Testaments; the Canadian oak chair, a gift from the city of Marseille; the ivory Christ who faces it; the great organ from the Cavaillé Coll workshops (25 pipes). There are fifteen chapels. The most beautiful are those of the Sacred Heart, of

Our Lady of Mount Carmel, of Saint Joseph. Their windows picture the apparitions; the confessionals are in Pyrenean oak.

To visit the treasure, approach the sacristy. You will see there a monstrance weighing 35 pounds and measuring four and a half feet. This unique piece of goldsmithing is the work of M. A. Calliat of Lyon.

We go down into the underground church, carved into the rock, and the scene changes. And eternal half-light reigns; it is the place of recollection par excellence. The pillars, the columns, intersect, lights flicker in the twenty-three lamps that are lit day and night. In the middle is the altar of the Holy Virgin, surrounded by chapels whose walls are covered with hearts of gold, silver, and vermeil.

The floor of the church is level with that of the Grotto. Two magnificent circular ramps, rising in the shape of a horseshoe, form in front of the entry a vast space with the most impressive effect. They will come to the entrance of the Basilica by bypassing the dome. This sanctuary, built according to the plans of M. Hardy, does not have a well-defined style; it is close to the Byzantine, but everything is mixed with it. Before entering admire the group formed by Saint Dominic receiving the rosary from the hands of the Mother of God.

The interior is shaped like a rotunda; there is not a pillar, not a stained glass window. Fifteen chapels, representing the fifteen mysteries of the rosary, surround the hemicircle.

The walls are covered with ex-votos as in the Crypt and Basilica. An oak parquet replaces the usual paving. The church is 157 feet long, 170 feet wide. All of the interior decoration is yet to be done. Offerings have been given by the faithful to build the high altar and the organ, but they are still not enough to do much.

The year 1896 saw some great progress achieved. Electricity was installed in the three churches. Before long, the Esplanade and the dock on the Gave would be illuminated in the same way.

A beautiful marble staircase connected the Rosary and the Basilica. The house of the Reverend Fathers of the Immaculate Conception is west of the Massabielle rocks, beside the Basilica. The Episcopal Palace rises farther on, in the midst of the Spélugues.

Under the Spélugues, to the southwest of Lourdes, are three openings, forming two chambers, today transformed into chapels and enclosed by a grill. Note in the room on the left of the marble altar the descent from the cross that is above. In the second room, the statue of Mary Magdalen.

After a thousand detours, a road leads up to the top of the Spélugues hill: it is the Calvary (328 feet). An altar with Christ and thirteen crosses, dominated in height by the cedarwood one from Jerusalem, form the fourteen stations.

The hospice of Our Lady of Sorrows, owing to the charity of Mlle. Saint-Frai, in religion Sister Saint-Jean-Baptiste, has been built on the Avenue de la Grotte. It receives a hundred of elderly infirm. During the pilgrimages, 500 ill people can be crowded in there.

The Grotto is surrounded by numerous convents: that of the Poor Clares is found on the Avenue de la Grotte; the monastery of the Carmelites, on the route de Pau; the Assumptionists on the same height but below the railway line; the Dominicans, close to the Visens hills; and the Sisters of the Immaculate Conception have built a superb house five minutes from the Basilica, behind the Episcopal Palace, on the Forest Road. They board pious women who want to avoid the noise of the city and hotels. Perpetual adoration has been established in their chapel.

Bernard Dauberive

The magnificent chapel requested by the Queen of Heaven was built.

IMMACULATE CONCEPTION

PROCLAMATION OF THE DOGMA OF THE IMMACULATE CONCEPTION

Pope Blessed Pius IX

Apostolic Constitution Ineffabilis Deus, *December 8, 1854*

Statement of the Church's sense[1]

God Ineffable—whose ways are mercy and truth, whose will is omnipotence itself, and whose wisdom "reaches from end to end mightily, and orders all things sweetly"—having foreseen from all eternity the lamentable wretchedness of the entire human race which would result from the sin of Adam, decreed, by a plan hidden from the centuries, to complete the first work of his goodness by a mystery yet more wondrously sublime through the Incarnation of the Word. This he decreed in order that man, who, contrary to the plan of Divine Mercy, had been led into sin by the cunning malice of Satan, should not perish; and in order that what had been lost in the first Adam would be gloriously restored in the Second Adam. From the very beginning, and before time began, the eternal Father chose and prepared for his only begotten Son a Mother in whom the Son of God would become incarnate and from whom, in the blessed fullness of time, he would be born into this world. Above all creatures did God so love her that truly in her was the Father well pleased with singular delight. Therefore, far above all the angels and all the saints so wondrously did God endow her with the abundance of all heavenly gifts poured from the treasury of his divinity that this mother, ever absolutely free of all stain of sin, all fair and perfect,

---

1. This translation of the text has been taken from the Papal Encyclical website at: https://www.papalencyclicals.net/pius09/p9ineff.htm. The paragraph headings have been added in order to facilitate reading. The doctrinal and historical notes by Abbé Alphonse David are in the 1953 Bonne Presse edition, with the *Nihil obstat: Paris, October 8, 1953*, and *Imprimatur Paris, October 12, 1953*, Michel Potevin, v.g.

would possess that fullness of holy innocence and sanctity than which, under God, one cannot even imagine anything greater, and which, outside of God, no mind can succeed in comprehending fully.

Supreme reason for this privilege: The divine motherhood

And, indeed, it was wholly fitting that so wonderful a mother should be ever resplendent with the glory of most sublime holiness and so completely free from all taint of original sin that she would triumph utterly over the ancient serpent. To her did the Father will to give his only begotten Son—the Son whom, equal to the Father and begotten by him, the Father loves from his heart—and to give this Son in such a way that

he would be the one and the same common Son of God the Father and of the Blessed Virgin Mary. It was she whom the Son himself chose to make his Mother, and it was from her that the Holy Spirit willed and brought it about that he should be conceived and born from whom he himself proceeds.[2]

Its degree of certainty: It is a revealed truth

The Catholic Church, directed by the Holy Spirit of God, is the pillar and base of truth and has ever held as divinely revealed and as contained in the deposit of heavenly revelation this doctrine concerning the original innocence of the august Virgin—a doctrine which is so perfectly in harmony with her wonderful sanctity and preeminent dignity as Mother of God—and thus has never ceased to explain, to teach, and to foster this doctrine age after age in many ways and by solemn acts. From this very doctrine, flourishing and wondrously propagated in the Catholic world through the efforts and zeal of the bishops, was made very clear by the Church when she did not hesitate to present for the public devotion and veneration of the faithful the Feast of the Conception of the Blessed Virgin.[3] By this most significant fact, the Church made it clear indeed that the conception of Mary is to be venerated as something extraordinary, wonderful, eminently holy, and different from the conception of all other human beings—for the

---

2. A number of theologians have drawn from these words the argument affirming that the grace in Mary, from the moment of her Immaculate Conception (initial grace), was greater not only than the grace of each of the angels and saints at their end (final grace), but also than this same final grace of all angels and all saints taken together. (See Garrigou- Lagrange, O.P.: *Mariologie, la Mère du Sauveur et notre vie intérieure* [Édit. De l'Abeille, 1941], p. 67.)

3. In the East, the feast began to exist at least as early as the end of the seventh century on December 9, under the names of the Annunciation of the Conception of the Mother of God, then of Conception of the Mother of God, with Mary having been conceived immaculate being the principal theme in the liturgy and homilies. In the West, it appeared

Church celebrates only the feast days of the saints. And hence the very words with which the Sacred Scriptures speak of Uncreated Wisdom and set forth his eternal origin, the Church, both in her ecclesiastical offices and in her liturgy, has been wont to apply likewise to the origin of the Blessed Virgin, inasmuch as God, by one and the same decree, had established the origin of Mary and the Incarnation of Divine Wisdom.

PROOF OF THE REVELATION OF THE IMMACULATE CONCEPTION

The Ordinary Teaching of the Church

These truths, so generally accepted and put into practice by the faithful, indicate how zealously

on different successive dates (December 9 or 8; May); in southern Italy (ninth century); in Ireland (ninth and tenth centuries), in England and Spain (eleventh century); in Normandy and Lyon and in numerous dioceses in France and Germany (twelfth century).... We could say that by the end of the fourteenth and beginning of the fifteenth century the feast was celebrated nearly universally. The popes first authorized it, then participated in it during their stay in Avignon (1309–1377) and on their return to Rome, and finally adopted it (fourteenth century). By the Bull *Commissi nobis* (December 6, 1708), Pope Clement XI imposed it on the whole Church: "By apostolic authority and the content of this document, We decree, ordain, and mandate that the feast of the Immaculate Conception of the Blessed Virgin Mary be henceforth observed and celebrated in all places, like other holy days of obligation, by all the faithful of both sexes and that it be inserted into the number of feasts that it is mandatory to observe."

the Roman Church, mother and teacher of all Churches, has continued to teach this doctrine of the Immaculate Conception of the Virgin. Yet the more important actions of the Church deserve to be mentioned in detail. For such dignity and authority belong to the Church that she alone is the center of truth and of Catholic unity. It is the Church in which alone religion has been inviolably preserved and from which all other Churches must receive the tradition of the Faith.

The same Roman Church, therefore, desired nothing more than by the most persuasive means to state, to protect, to promote and to defend the doctrine of the Immaculate Conception. This fact is most clearly shown to the whole world by numerous and significant acts of the Roman Pontiffs, our predecessors. To them, in the person of the Prince of the Apostles, were divinely entrusted by Christ our Lord, the charge and supreme care and the power of feeding the lambs and sheep; in particular, of confirming their brethren, and of ruling and governing the universal Church.

Her teaching on the veneration

Our predecessors, indeed, by virtue of their apostolic authority, gloried in instituting the Feast of the Conception in the Roman Church. They did so to enhance its importance and dignity by a suitable Office and Mass, whereby the prerogative of the Virgin, her exception from the hereditary taint, was most distinctly affirmed. As to the homage already instituted, they spared no effort to promote and to extend it either by the granting of indulgences, or by allowing cities, provinces and kingdoms to choose as their patroness God's own Mother, under the title of "The Immaculate Conception". Again, our predecessors approved confraternities, congregations, and religious communities founded in honor of the Immaculate Conception, monasteries, hospitals, altars, or churches; they praised persons who vowed to uphold with all their ability the doctrine of the Immaculate Conception of the Mother of God. Besides, it afforded the greatest joy to our predecessors to ordain that the Feast of the Conception should be celebrated in every church with the very same honor as the Feast of the Nativity; that it should be celebrated with an octave by the whole Church; that it should be reverently and generally observed as a holy day of obligation; and that a pontifical Capella should be held in our Liberian pontifical basilica on the day dedicated to the conception of the Virgin.

Finally, in their desire to impress this doctrine of the Immaculate Conception of the Mother of God upon the hearts of the faithful, and to intensify the people's piety and enthusiasm for the homage and the veneration of the Virgin conceived without the stain of original sin, they delighted to grant, with the greatest pleasure, permission to proclaim the Immaculate Conception of the Virgin in the Litany of Loreto, and in the Preface of the Mass, so that the rule of prayer might thus serve to illustrate the rule of belief. Therefore, we ourselves, following the procedure of our predecessors, have not only approved and accepted what had already been established, but bearing in mind, moreover, the decree of Sixtus IV,[4] have confirmed by our authority a proper Office in

---

4. The first papal solemn documents in favor of the feast and the doctrine of the Immaculate Conception date from Pope Sixtus IV (1471–1484). On April 29, 1476, by his Constitution *Cum praeexcelsa*, Pope Sixtus IV approved and recommended the proper office of the Conception written by the Friar Minor Léonard de Nogarole, and on October 4, 1480, by the Letter *Libenter ad ea*, another office by the Franciscan Bernardin de Busti. Finally, in 1482 and 1483, by the

honor of the Immaculate Conception, and have with exceeding joy extended its use to the universal Church.[5]

Her teaching on the doctrine

Now inasmuch as whatever pertains to sacred worship is intimately connected with its object and cannot have either consistency or durability if this object is vague or uncertain, our predecessors, the Roman Pontiffs, therefore, while directing all their efforts toward an increase of the devotion to the conception, made it their aim not only to emphasize the object with the utmost zeal, but also to enunciate the exact doctrine.[6] Definitely and clearly they taught that the feast was held in honor of the conception of the Virgin. They denounced as false and absolutely foreign to the mind of the Church the opinion of those who held and affirmed that it was not the conception of the Virgin but her sanctification that was

Bull *Grave nimis*, Sixtus IV brought censures against those who were accusing of heresy the proponents of the Immaculate Conception and its feast. After Sixtus IV, the pontifical acts in favor of the Immaculate Conception multiplied: "Except for those who reigned for a very short time, the twenty-five popes who governed the Church during this period of around two centuries (1486–1667) nearly all manifested their devotion to the Immaculate Virgin by their acts in her favor; very numerous acts that will be found enumerated in detail in a Bull, *Mulierem pulchram*, that Benedict XIV had prepared but which was not published." (X Le Bachelet, *Diction. de théol. Cath.*, vol. 7, col. 1164.) Under these conditions, it is difficult to explain the remark by G. Herzog: "When one goes through the series of pontifical acts relating to the Conception of the Virgin, the first impression that one experiences is that of astonishment. What one pope does another undoes; the work of one evening is destroyed the next day: you find yourself in the presence of Penelope's shroud" (quoted by Le Bachelet, *Diction. de théol. Cath.*, vol. 7, col. 1188).

5. Decree of the Sacred Congregation of Rites, September 30, 1847.

6. There is an obvious difference. Sanctification, which is to say, union with God through grace, and the Immaculate Conception are not synonymous: Saint John the Baptist was sanctified before his birth; he was not immaculate in his conception. The two expressions would signify the same thing only on the condition of specifying that Mary was sanctified already in the first instant of her Conception. And such was not the intention of those who were speaking of the sanctification of Mary rather than of her Immaculate Conception. Already, as early as the thirteenth century, those who did not believe it possible to subscribe to the Immaculate Conception of Mary, because of the universality of the Redemption, had reduced the feast of the Conception to the idea of sanctification. According to their interpretation, the sanctification of Mary was celebrated on the day of her Conception because it was not known when the precise moment of that sanctification took place. (See St. Thomas, *Summa Theologia*, III, q. 27, art. 2, 3 resp.)

was not that of the first instance of conception but the second. In fact, they held it was their duty not only to uphold and defend with all their power the Feast of the Conception of the Blessed Virgin but also to assert that the true object of this veneration was her conception considered in its first instant.

Hence the words of one of our predecessors, Alexander VII, who authoritatively and decisively declared the mind of the Church:

"Concerning the most Blessed Virgin Mary, Mother of God, ancient indeed is that devotion of the faithful based on the belief that her soul, in the first instant of its creation and in the first instant of the soul's infusion into the body, was, by a special grace and privilege of God, in view of the merits of Jesus Christ, her Son and the Redeemer of the human race, preserved free from all stain of original sin. And in this sense have the faithful ever solemnized and celebrated the Feast of the Conception."[7]

Moreover, our predecessors considered it their special solemn duty with all diligence, zeal, and effort to preserve intact the doctrine of the Immaculate Conception of the Mother of God. For, not only have they in no way ever allowed this doctrine to be censured or changed, but they have gone much further and by clear statements repeatedly asserted that the doctrine by which we profess the Immaculate Conception of the Virgin is on its own merits entirely in harmony with the ecclesiastical veneration; that it is ancient and widespread, and of the same nature as that which the Roman Church has undertaken to

honored by the Church. They never thought that greater leniency should be extended toward those who, attempting to disprove the doctrine of the Immaculate Conception of the Virgin, devised a distinction between the first and second instance of conception and inferred that the conception which the Church celebrates

---

7. In order to save the principle of the Redemption of all men by Christ, some imagined, in fact, a first instant when Mary had been conceived with sin and a second instant immediately after when she had been sanctified. It was in this sense, they thought, that one could preach and celebrate the Immaculate Conception: the second instant following immediately on the first, one would not distinguish them in practice. In reality, this was to deny the privilege of the Immaculate Conception such as it had been conceived by the Church: Mary never existed with sin.

promote and to protect, and that it is entirely worthy to be used in the Sacred Liturgy and solemn prayers. Not content with this they most strictly prohibited any opinion contrary to this doctrine to be defended in public or private in order that the doctrine of the Immaculate Conception of the Virgin might remain inviolate. By repeated blows they wished to put an end to such an opinion. And lest these oft-repeated and clearest statements seem useless, they added a sanction to them.

All these things our illustrious predecessor, Alexander VII,[8] summed up in these words: We have in mind the fact that the Holy Roman Church solemnly celebrated the Feast of the Conception of the undefiled and ever-Virgin Mary, and has long ago appointed for this a special and proper Office according to the pious, devout, and laudable instruction which was given by our predecessor, Sixtus IV.[9] Likewise, we were desirous, after the example of our predecessors, to favor this praiseworthy piety, devotion, feast and veneration—a veneration which is in keeping with the piety unchanged in the Roman Church from the day it was instituted. We also desired to protect this piety and devotion of venerating and extolling the most Blessed Virgin preserved from original sin by the grace of the Holy Spirit. Moreover, we were anxious to preserve the unity of the Spirit in the bond of peace in the flock of Christ by putting down arguments and controversies and

by removing scandals. So at the instance and request of the bishops mentioned above, with the chapters of the churches, and of King Philip[10] and his kingdoms, we renew

---

8. The Constitution *Sollicitudo omnium ecclesiarum* of December 8, 1661. With Sixtus IV and up to the dogmatic definition (1854), Alexander VII is one of three popes who did the most for the Immaculate Conception: Sixtus IV officially approved the feast (1476); Alexander VII determined the proper object of it: the Immaculate Conception (1661); Clement XI extended the feast to the universal Church (1708).

9. See note 3 above.

10. In 1659, the king of Spain, Philip IV, had sent to Rome Louis Crespi de Borgia, bishop of Plasencia, with the mission of asking the pope for a declaration about the proper object of the worship of the Conception of Mary, which is to say, about her actual Conception free from original sin, and not about her sanctification.

> " At this spring where gentle Bernadette was the first to go to drink and wash, all miseries of soul and body will flow away. "

BOTTLES

of the doctrine asserting that the soul of the Blessed Virgin, in its creation and infusion into the body, was endowed with the grace of the Holy Spirit and preserved from original sin; and also in favor of the feast and veneration of the conception of the Virgin Mother of God, which, as is manifest, was instituted in keeping with that pious belief. So we command this feast to be observed under the censures and penalties contained in the same Constitutions.

And therefore, against all and every one of those who shall continue to construe the said Constitutions and Decrees in a manner apt to frustrate the favor which is thereby given to the said doctrine, and to the feast and relative veneration, or who shall dare to call into question the said sentence, feast and worship, or in any way whatever, directly or indirectly, shall declare themselves opposed to it under any pretext whatsoever, were it but only to the extent of examining the possibilities of effecting the definition, or who shall comment upon and interpret the Sacred Scripture, or the Fathers or Doctors in connection therewith, or finally, for any reason, or on any occasion, shall dare, either in writing or verbally, to speak, preach, treat, dispute or determine upon, or assert whatsoever against the foregoing matters, or who shall adduce any arguments against them, while leaving them unresolved, or who shall disagree therewith in any other conceivable manner, we hereby declare that in addition to the penalties and censures contained in the Constitutions issued by Sixtus IV to which we

the Constitutions and Decrees issued by the Roman Pontiffs, our predecessors, especially Sixtus IV,[11] Paul V,[12] and Gregory XV,[13] in favor

---

11. See note 3 above.

12. The Constitution *Sanctissimus* of September 12, 1617. Paul V ordered among other things "not to allow oneself in the future, in preaching lessons, conclusions, and other acts of any nature, to affirm publicly, until there is definition or derogation on the part of His Holiness or the Apostolic See, that the Blessed Virgin was conceived in original sin."

13. The Constitution *Sanctissimus* of June 4, 1622. Gregory XV extended the defense brought by his predecessor Paul V to sermons and private writings and gave the order to celebrate the Conception of Mary as the Roman Church did, which is to say, "not to use any term other than that of Conception at Mass and the Divine Office, public or private."

want them to be subjected and to which we subject them by the present Constitution, we hereby decree that they be deprived of the authority of preaching, reading in public, that is to say teaching and interpreting; and that they be also deprived ipso facto of the power of voting, either actively or passively, in all elections, without the need for any further declaration; and that also, ipso facto, without any further declaration, they shall incur the penalty of perpetual disability from preaching, reading in public, teaching and interpreting, and that it shall not be possible to absolve them from such penalty, or remove it, save through ourselves, or the Roman Pontiffs who shall succeed us. We also require that the same shall remain subject to any other penalties which by us, of our own free will—or by the Roman Pontiffs, our successors (according as they may decree)—shall be deemed advisable to establish, and by the present Constitution we declare them subject thereto, and hereby renew the above Decrees and Constitutions of Paul V and Gregory XV.

Moreover, as regards those books in which the said sentence, feast and relative veneration are called into question or are contradicted in any way whatsoever, according to what has already been stated, either in writing or verbally, in discourses, sermons, lectures, treatises and debates—that may have been printed after the above-praised Decree of Paul V, or may be printed hereafter we hereby prohibit them, subject to the penalties and censures established by the Index of prohibited books, and ipso facto, without any further declaration, we desire and command that they be held as expressly prohibited.

All are aware with how much diligence this doctrine of the Immaculate Conception of the Mother of God has been handed down, proposed, and defended by the most outstanding religious orders, by the more celebrated theological academies,[14] and by very eminent doctors in the sciences of theology. All know,

14. Celebrated among all was the decision taken by the Sorbonne on March 3, 1496. By that decision, it was decreed that all those who applied for University degrees had to swear an oath to defend the Immaculate Conception of Mary, something it rigorously adhered to in the future.

likewise, how eager the bishops have been to profess openly and publicly, even in ecclesiastical assemblies, that Mary, the most holy Mother of God, by virtue of the foreseen merits of Christ, our Lord and Redeemer, was never subject to original sin, but was completely preserved from the original taint, and hence she was redeemed in a manner more sublime.

Besides, we must note a fact of the greatest importance indeed. Even the Council of Trent itself, when it promulgated the dogmatic decree concerning original sin, following the testimonies of the Sacred Scriptures, of the Holy Fathers and of the renowned Council, decreed and defined that all men are born infected by original sin; nevertheless, it solemnly declared that it had no intention of including the blessed and immaculate Virgin Mary, the Mother of God, in this decree and in the general extension of its definition. Indeed, considering the times and circumstances, the Fathers of Trent sufficiently intimated by this declaration that the Blessed Virgin Mary was free from the original stain; and thus they clearly signified that nothing could be reasonably cited from the Sacred Scriptures, from Tradition, or from the authority of the Fathers, which would in any way be opposed to so great a prerogative of the Blessed Virgin.[15]

The tradition of the Ancients and the Fathers.

And indeed, illustrious documents of venerable antiquity, of both the Eastern and the Western Church, very forcibly testify that this doctrine of the Immaculate Conception of the most Blessed Virgin, which was daily more and more splendidly explained, stated and confirmed by the highest authority, teaching, zeal, knowledge, and wisdom of the Church, and which was disseminated among all peoples and nations of the Catholic world in a marvelous manner—this doctrine always existed in the Church as a doctrine that has been received from our ancestors, and that has been stamped with the character of revealed doctrine. For the Church of Christ, watchful guardian that she is, and defender of the dogmas deposited with her, never changes anything, never diminishes anything, never adds anything to them; but with all diligence she treats the ancient documents faithfully and wisely; if they really are of ancient origin and if the faith of the Fathers has transmitted them, she strives to investigate and explain them in such a way that the ancient dogmas of heavenly doctrine will be made evident and clear, but will retain their full, integral, and proper

---

15. Historical circumstances emphasize the value of this interpretation of the thought of the Council of Trent (1546). The original text on the universal transmission of original sin, without being corrected, could have left doubt on the Immaculate Conception of Mary. In the debates that this occasioned, more than two-thirds of the members of the Assembly, beginning with its first president, Cardinal del Monte, proposed different additions so that it would be very apparent that the Holy Virgin was not included in this. The correction adopted, nevertheless, did not constitute a definition in itself; the Council Fathers had declared that they did not want to approach this problem.

nature, and will grow only within their own genus—that is, within the same dogma, in the same sense and the same meaning.[16]

Interpretation of the Protoevangelium

The Fathers and writers of the Church, well versed in the heavenly Scriptures, had nothing more at heart than to vie with one another in preaching and teaching in many wonderful ways the Virgin's supreme sanctity, dignity, and immunity from all stain of sin, and her renowned victory over the most foul enemy of the human race. This they did in the books they wrote to explain the Scriptures, to vindicate the dogmas, and to instruct the faithful. These ecclesiastical writers in quoting the words by which at the beginning of the world God announced his merciful remedies prepared for the regeneration of mankind—words by which he crushed the audacity of the deceitful serpent and wondrously raised up the hope of our race, saying, "I will put enmities between you and the woman, between your seed and her seed" (Gen 3:15)—taught that by this divine prophecy the

16. These lines indicate perfectly the role of the Church; she does not create Tradition, in which, as in Scripture, are contained the truths revealed by God: "She changes nothing in it, does not take anything away from it, adds nothing to it." She gives the authentic meaning of it in the most precise forms: "In such a way that these ancient dogmas of heavenly doctrine receive clarity, light, distinction, while keeping their fullness, their integrity, their own character."

The drafting of the Bull of Pius IX should also be noted well. His text "contains two clearly distinct phrases: the first, a narrative, in which is attributed to the Fathers and ecclesiastical writers the aforementioned teaching, *docuere* (they taught); the second, a deduction, *quocirca* (this is why), in which the Fathers are no longer directly on stage; it is the editors of the Bull and Pius IX along with them, who, going beyond the teachings of the Fathers, who provide the principle, draw the consequences from them and apply them" (Le Bachelet, *Diction. de théol. Cath.*, col. 860).

merciful Redeemer of mankind, Jesus Christ, the only begotten Son of God, was clearly foretold: That his most Blessed Mother, the Virgin Mary, was prophetically indicated; and, at the same time, the very enmity of both against the evil one was significantly expressed. Hence, just as Christ, the Mediator between God and man, assumed human nature, blotted the handwriting of the decree that stood against us, and fastened it triumphantly to the cross, so the most holy Virgin, united with him by a most intimate and indissoluble bond, was, with him and through him, eternally at enmity with the evil serpent, and most completely triumphed

Nothing is hopeless [under the protection of the One who bears] toward us a truly motherly affection.

over him, and thus crushed his head with her immaculate foot.[17]

This sublime and singular privilege of the Blessed Virgin, together with her most excellent innocence, purity, holiness and freedom from every stain of sin, as well as the unspeakable abundance and greatness of all heavenly graces, virtues and privileges—these the Fathers beheld in that ark of Noah, which was built by divine command and escaped entirely safe and sound from the common shipwreck of the whole world (Gen 6–9); in the ladder which Jacob saw reaching from the earth to heaven, by whose rungs the angels of God ascended and descended, and on whose top the Lord himself leaned (Gen 28:12); in that

---

17. There would be no end to the multiple opinions given by commentators on the Protoevangelium. We will merely bring out the general idea that is important here: "The woman in Genesis and her lineage point, at least principally, to Mary and her divine Son, the enmity proclaimed and effectively willed by God is presented as common to both; it will be for the Mother as for the Son complete, absolute. It is that which gives to the plan of divine revenge all its meaning and all its scope; for the group of the conquered, Adam and Eve, is substituted the group of the conquerors, which is also composed of a man and a woman. The first Eve, repentant and raised up, has resumed, it is true, the hostilities against the serpent; but in this woman, at first defeated and not having recovered her original innocence, revenge can only be partial and relative; there will be total and absolute revenge only on the day when the primitive Eve, the one who left the Creator's hands completely pure, lives again, so to speak, in another herself and will find herself close to the New Adam for the supreme battle" (Le Bachelet, *Dict. de théol. Cath.*, vol. 7, col. 859).

bush which Moses saw in the holy place burning on all sides, which was not consumed or injured in any way but grew green and blossomed beautifully (Ex 3:2); in that impregnable tower before the enemy, from which hung a thousand bucklers and all the armor of the strong (Song 4:4); in that garden enclosed on all sides, which cannot be violated or corrupted by any deceitful plots (Song 4:12); as in that resplendent city of God, which has its foundations on the holy mountains (Song 86:1); in that most august temple of God, which, radiant with divine splendors, is full of the glory of God (Is 6:1–4); and in very many other biblical types of this kind. In such allusions the Fathers taught that the exalted dignity of the Mother of God, her spotless innocence and her sanctity unstained by any fault, had been prophesied in a wonderful manner.

The application of symbolic words

In like manner did they use the words of the prophets to describe this wondrous abundance of divine gifts and the original innocence of the Virgin of whom Jesus was born. They celebrated the august Virgin as the spotless dove, as the holy Jerusalem, as the exalted throne of God, as the ark and house of holiness which Eternal Wisdom built, and as that Queen who, abounding in delights and leaning on her Beloved, came forth from the mouth of the Most High, entirely perfect, beautiful, most dear to God and never stained with the least blemish.

The interpretation of the greeting of the Archangel Gabriel and of Elizabeth

When the Fathers and writers of the Church meditated on the fact that the most Blessed Virgin was, in the name and by order of God himself, proclaimed full of grace (Lk 1:28) by the Angel Gabriel when he announced her most sublime dignity of Mother of God, they thought that this singular and solemn salutation, never heard before, showed that the Mother of God is the seat of all divine graces and is adorned with all gifts of the Holy Spirit. To them Mary is an almost infinite treasury, an inexhaustible abyss of these gifts, to such an extent that she was never subject to the curse and was, together with her Son, the only partaker of perpetual benediction. Hence she was worthy to hear Elizabeth, inspired by the Holy Spirit, exclaim: "Blessed are you among women, and blessed is the fruit of your womb" (Lk 1:42).[18]

Mary compared with Eve

Hence, it is the clear and unanimous opinion of the Fathers that the most glorious Virgin, for whom "he who is mighty has done great things", was resplendent with such an abundance of heavenly gifts, with such a fullness of grace and with such innocence, that she is an unspeakable miracle of God—indeed, the crown of all miracles and truly the Mother of God; that she approaches as near to God himself as is possible for a created being; and that she is above all men and angels in glory. Hence, to demonstrate the original innocence and sanctity of the Mother of God, not only did they frequently compare her to Eve while yet a virgin, while yet innocent, while yet incorrupt, while

not yet deceived by the deadly snares of the most treacherous serpent; but they have also exalted her above Eve with a wonderful variety of expressions. Eve listened to the serpent with lamentable consequences; she fell from original innocence and became his slave. The most Blessed Virgin, on the contrary, ever increased her original gift, and not only never lent an ear to the serpent, but by divinely given power she utterly destroyed the force and dominion of the evil one.

Images or metaphors

Accordingly, the Fathers have never ceased to call the Mother of God the lily among thorns, the land entirely intact, the Virgin undefiled, immaculate, ever blessed, and free from all contagion of sin, she from whom was formed the new Adam, the flawless, brightest, and most beautiful paradise of innocence, immortality and delights planted by God himself and protected against all the snares of the poisonous serpent, the incorruptible wood that the worm of sin had never corrupted, the fountain ever clear and sealed with the power of the Holy Spirit, the most holy temple, the treasure of immortality, the one and only daughter of life—not of death—the plant not of anger but of grace, through the singular Providence of God growing ever green contrary to the common law, coming as it does from a corrupted and tainted root.

---

18. Along with the protoevangelium, the twofold greetings of Gabriel and Elizabeth are the second proof from Sacred Scripture brought by theologians in favor of the Immaculate Conception. But, like the first, it is so above all through Tradition, which has interpreted it in this sense. In other words, this twofold greeting would not be sufficient, considered independently, to prove the privilege: but it proves it if one takes into consideration the interpretation of the Fathers. For them, Jesus and Mary are united in the same divine blessing, and the fullness of grace is not found in Mary only at the moment when she becomes Mother; it has always existed in her as a prerequisite condition for her divine motherhood and her role. It is remarkable that the Bull *Ineffabilis* presents these two texts, the protoevangelium and the greeting, in proof of the Tradition, the only one invoked directly by Pius IX. "In the Bull that contains the definition of the mystery, Pius IX did not insist on the testimonies of Scripture as if they formed a separate argument; rather, he links them, if I may speak this way, to the testimonies of the Fathers who determined their meaning" (Bishop Malou: *L'Immaculée Conception* [1857], 1:246).

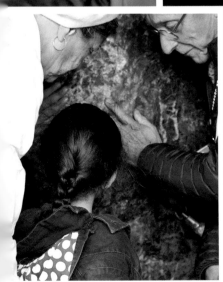

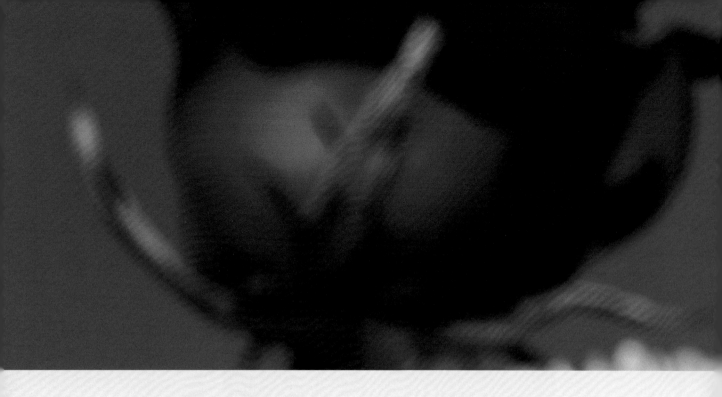

Explicit affirmations

As if these splendid eulogies and tributes were not sufficient, the Fathers proclaimed with particular and definite statements that when one treats of sin, the holy Virgin Mary is not even to be mentioned; for to her more grace was given than was necessary to conquer sin completely.[19] They also declared that the most glorious Virgin was Reparatrix of the first parents, the giver of life to posterity; that she was chosen before the ages, prepared for himself by the Most High, foretold by God when he said to the serpent, "I will put enmities between you and the woman" (Gen 3:15), unmistakable evidence that she has crushed the poisonous head of the serpent. And hence they affirmed that the Blessed Virgin was, through grace, entirely free from every stain of sin, and from all corruption of body, soul and mind; that she was always united with God and joined to him by an eternal covenant; that she was never in darkness but always in light; and that, therefore, she was entirely a fit habitation for Christ, not because of the state of her body, but because of her original grace.

Universal expressions of supereminent holiness

To these praises they have added very noble words. Speaking of the conception of the Virgin, they testified that nature yielded to grace and, unable to go on, stood trembling. The Virgin Mother of God would not be conceived by Anne before grace would bear its fruits; it was proper that she be conceived as the firstborn, by whom "the firstborn of every creature"

19. Reference to the words of Saint Augustine, who, after having rejected the assertions of Pelagius about certain persons who supposedly lived absolutely without any sin, adds "with the exception of the Holy Virgin, about whom I do not want there to be any question with regard to sins, and that for the honor of the Lord: that she had in fact received a superabundant grace to obtain absolute victory over sin we know from the fact the she merited to conceive and give birth to the One who was incontestably without sin" (On Nature and Grace, chap. XXXVI, PL 44:267). Even if Saint Augustine speaks here only of personal sins, he nevertheless affirms that Mary is exempt from all sin, for the honor of the Lord, and original sin in Mary would be no less of an attack on the honor of the Lord.

would be conceived. They testified, too, that the flesh of the Virgin, although derived from Adam, did not contract the stains of Adam, and that on this account the most Blessed Virgin was the tabernacle created by God himself and formed by the Holy Spirit, truly a work in royal purple, adorned and woven with gold, which that new Bezalel (Ex 31:2) made. They affirmed that the same Virgin is, and is deservedly, the first and especial work of God, escaping the fiery arrows of the evil one; that she is beautiful by nature and entirely free from all stain; that at her Immaculate Conception she came into the world all radiant like the dawn. For it was certainly not fitting that this vessel of election should be wounded by the common injuries, since she, differing so much from the others, had only nature in common with them, not sin. In fact, it was quite fitting that, as the Only Begotten has a Father in heaven, whom the Seraphim extol as thrice holy, so he should have a Mother on earth who would never be without the splendor of holiness.

This doctrine so filled the minds and souls of our ancestors in the faith that a singular and truly marvelous style of speech came into vogue among them. They have frequently addressed the Mother of God as immaculate, as immaculate in every respect; innocent, and verily most innocent; spotless, and entirely spotless; holy and removed from every stain of sin; all pure, all stainless, the very model of purity and innocence; more beautiful than beauty, more lovely than loveliness; more holy than holiness, singularly holy and most pure in soul and body; the one who surpassed all integrity and virginity; the only one who has become the dwelling place of all the graces of the most Holy Spirit. God alone excepted, Mary is more excellent than all, and by nature fair and beautiful, and more holy than the Cherubim and Seraphim.[20] To praise her all the tongues of heaven and earth do not suffice.

20. A number of these expressions from paragraphs 6 and 8 were repeated by Pius XII in his encyclical *Fulgens Corona* of September 8, 1953.

and most beautiful dove, as a rose ever blooming, as perfectly pure, ever immaculate, and ever blessed. She is celebrated as innocence never sullied and as the second Eve who brought forth the Emmanuel.

The Dogmatic Definition of the Immaculate Conception

Old and new petitions

No wonder, then, that the Pastors of the Church and the faithful gloried daily more and more in professing with so much piety, religion, and love this doctrine of the Immaculate Conception of the Virgin Mother of God, which, as the Fathers discerned, was recorded in the Divine Scriptures; which was handed down in so many of their most important writings; which was expressed and celebrated in so many illustrious monuments of venerable antiquity; which was proposed and confirmed by the official and authoritative teaching of the Church. Hence, nothing was dearer, nothing more pleasing to these pastors than to venerate, invoke, and proclaim with most ardent affection the Virgin Mother of God conceived without original stain. Accordingly, from ancient times the bishops of the Church, ecclesiastics, religious orders, and even emperors and kings, have earnestly petitioned this Apostolic See to define as a dogma of the Catholic Faith the Immaculate Conception of the most holy Mother of God.[21] These petitions were renewed in these our own times; they were especially brought to the attention of Gregory XVI, our

Everyone is cognizant that this style of speech has passed almost spontaneously into the books of the most holy liturgy and the Offices of the Church, in which they occur so often and abundantly. In them, the Mother of God is invoked and praised as the one spotless

---

21. The request of the bishops in favor of a dogmatic definition go back at least to the beginning of the fifteenth century, as can be seen from the Council of Basel (1439). As for the heads of state, already at the beginning of the seventeenth century, Philip II, king of Spain, began to approach the Holy See, then supported by the king of Poland, Sigismond III, with a view to obtaining the definition of the privilege. It is known that Spain, civil and religious, was always at the forefront in promoting the cult of the Immaculate Conception.

predecessor of happy memory,[22] and to ourselves, not only by bishops, but by the secular clergy and religious orders, by sovereign rulers and by the faithful.[23]

The immediate preparation

Mindful, indeed, of all these things and considering them most attentively with particular joy in our heart, as soon as we, by the inscrutable design of Providence, had been raised to the sublime Chair of St. Peter—in spite of our unworthiness—and had begun to govern the universal Church, nothing have we had more at heart—a heart which from our tenderest years has overflowed with devoted veneration and love for the most Blessed Virgin—than to show forth her prerogatives in resplendent light.

That we might proceed with great prudence, we established a special congregation of our venerable brethren, the cardinals of the holy Roman Church, illustrious for their piety, wisdom, and knowledge of the sacred scriptures.[24] We also selected priests, both secular and regular, well trained in the theological sciences, that they should most carefully consider all matters pertaining to the Immaculate

---

22. It was thus that in 1840, ten French archbishops, those of Cambrai, Albi, Besançon, Bordeaux, Sens, Avignon, Auch, Reims, Bourges, and Lyon, and forty-one of their suffragan bishops signed and addressed to Pope Gregory XVI a collective letter in favor of the definition. From 1843 to 1845, the same pope received from bishops of other countries some forty similar supplications. The Manifestation of the Miraculous Medal, rue du Bac (1830), and the conversion of Alphonse Ratisbonne (1842) in Saint-André delle Fratte, were not unrelated to this outbreak of new petitions. Pope Gregory XVI, despite his devotion to the Immaculate One—he declared himself ready to shed his blood to the last drop in order to bear witness to and seal this glorious privilege—did not consider it necessary to act on these requests for reasons of expediency because of the reluctance of certain countries: Germany, England, Ireland....

23. From the beginning of the pontificate of Pius IX, a hundred new petitions continued to arrive in Rome, of which seventy were from Italian prelates, eleven from the papal states, and one from Ferdinand II, king of the two Sicilies.

24. This pre-preparatory Congregation, composed of eight cardinals and five consultors, was named by Pius IX during his stay in Gaète, on December 6, 1848. It was held at Naples on December 22, under the presidency of Cardinal Lambruschini. All proclaimed themselves in favor of the definition, but unanimity was not achieved with respect to the way chosen to define it.

Conception of the Virgin and make known to us their opinion.[25]

Although we knew the mind of the bishops from the petitions which we had received from them, namely, that the Immaculate Conception of the Blessed Virgin be finally defined, nevertheless, on February 2, 1849,[26] we sent an Encyclical Letter from Gaeta to all our venerable brethren, the bishops of the Catholic world, that they should offer prayers to God and then tell us in writing what the piety and devotion of their faithful was in regard to the Immaculate Conception of the Mother of God. We likewise inquired what the bishops themselves thought about defining this doctrine and what their wishes were in regard to making known with all possible solemnity our supreme judgment.

We were certainly filled with the greatest consolation when the replies of our venerable brethren came to us. For, replying to us with a most enthusiastic joy, exultation and zeal, they not only again confirmed their own singular piety toward the Immaculate Conception of the most Blessed Virgin, and that of the secular and religious clergy and of the faithful, but with one voice they even entreated us to define by our supreme judgment and authority the Immaculate Conception of the Virgin.[27]

25. This council of theologians was instituted by Pius IX on June 1, 1848. It was composed of twenty members: prelates of the Roman Congregations, religious from various Orders, and several renowned masters. Only three were unfavorable to the definition. In 1850 and 1851, three and then six more were added, of whom only one declared himself against the definition.

26. The encyclical *Ubi Primum*, which the Congregation, held in Naples, had suggested to Pope Pius IX.

27. Of the 603 responses of this kind of council "through writing", as this referendum was called, 546 bishops, a little more than nine-tenths, declared themselves expressly for the definition. The others opposed it, particularly because of questions of expediency. Only four or five bishops declared themselves categorically against the whole dogmatic definition.

In the meantime we were indeed filled with no less joy when, after a diligent examination, our venerable brethren, the cardinals of the special congregation and the theologians chosen by us as counselors (whom we mentioned above), asked with the same enthusiasm and fervor for the definition of the Immaculate Conception of the Mother of God.[28]

Consequently, following the examples of our predecessors, and desiring to proceed in the traditional manner, we announced and held a consistory, in which we addressed our brethren, the cardinals of the Holy Roman Church. It was the greatest spiritual joy for us when we heard them ask us to promulgate the dogmatic definition of the Immaculate Conception of the Virgin Mother of God.[29]

Therefore, having full trust in the Lord that the opportune time had come for defining the Immaculate Conception of the Blessed Virgin Mary, Mother of God, which Holy Scripture, venerable Tradition, the constant mind of the Church, the desire of Catholic bishops and the faithful, and the memorable Acts and Constitutions of our predecessors, wonderfully illustrate and proclaim, and having most diligently considered all things, as we poured forth to God ceaseless and fervent prayers, we concluded that we should no longer delay in decreeing and defining by our supreme authority the Immaculate Conception of the Blessed Virgin. And thus, we can satisfy the most holy desire of the Catholic world as well as our own devotion toward the most holy Virgin, and at the same time honor more and more the only begotten Son, Jesus Christ our Lord through his holy Mother—since whatever honor and

28. See notes 22 and 23 for the responses of the Congregation of cardinals and those of the council of theologians.

29. Pius IX held this secret Consistory on December 1, 1854.

praise are bestowed on the Mother redound to the Son.

The dogmatic definition

Wherefore, in humility and fasting, we unceasingly offered our private prayers as well as the public prayers of the Church to God the Father through his Son, that he would deign to direct and strengthen our mind by the power of the Holy Spirit. In like manner did we implore the help of the entire heavenly host as we ardently invoked the Paraclete. Accordingly, by the inspiration of the Holy Spirit, for the honor of the Holy and undivided Trinity, for the glory and adornment of the Virgin Mother of God, for the exaltation of the Catholic Faith, and for the furtherance of the Catholic religion, by the authority of Jesus Christ our Lord, of the Blessed Apostles Peter and Paul, and by our own: "We declare, pronounce, and define that the doctrine which holds that the most Blessed Virgin Mary, in the first instance of her conception, by a singular grace and privilege granted by Almighty God, in view of the merits of Jesus Christ, the Savior of the human race, was preserved free from all stain of original sin, is a doctrine revealed by God and therefore to be believed firmly and constantly by all the faithful."[30]

Hence, if anyone shall dare—which God forbid!—to think otherwise than as has been defined by us, let him know and understand that he is condemned by his own judgment; that he has suffered shipwreck in the faith; that he has separated from the unity of the Church; and that, furthermore, by his own action he incurs the penalties established by law if he should dare to express in words or writing or by any other outward means the errors he thinks in his heart.

Hoped-for results

Our soul overflows with joy and our tongue with exultation. We give, and we shall continue to give, the humblest and deepest thanks to Jesus Christ, our Lord, because through his singular grace he has granted to us, unworthy though we be, to decree and offer this honor and glory and praise to his most holy Mother. All our hope do we repose in the most Blessed Virgin—in the all fair and immaculate one who has crushed the poisonous head of the most cruel serpent and brought salvation to the world: in her who is the glory of the prophets and apostles, the honor of the martyrs, the crown and joy of all the saints; in her who is the safest refuge and the most trustworthy helper of all who are in danger; in her who, with her only begotten Son, is the most powerful Mediatrix and Conciliatrix in the whole world; in her who is the most excellent glory, ornament, and impregnable stronghold of the holy Church; in her who has destroyed all heresies and snatched the faithful people and nations from all kinds of direst calamities; in her do we hope who has delivered us from so many threatening dangers. We have, therefore, a very certain hope and complete confidence that the most Blessed Virgin will ensure by her most powerful patronage that all difficulties be removed and all errors dissipated, so that our Holy Mother the Catholic Church may flourish daily more and more throughout all the nations and countries, and may reign "from sea to sea and from the river to the ends of the earth", and may enjoy genuine peace,

---

30. We are stressing in the Bull what constitutes the dogmatic definition per se, which alone is guaranteed by the infallibility of the Pope and demands our faith.

tranquility and liberty. We are firm in our confidence that she will obtain pardon for the sinner, health for the sick, strength of heart for the weak, consolation for the afflicted, help for those in danger; that she will remove spiritual blindness from all who are in error, so that they may return to the path of truth and justice, and that there may be one flock and one shepherd.

Let all the children of the Catholic Church, who are so very dear to us, hear these words of ours. With a still more ardent zeal for piety, religion and love, let them continue to venerate, invoke, and pray to the most Blessed Virgin Mary, Mother of God, conceived without original sin. Let them fly with utter confidence to this most sweet Mother of mercy and grace in all dangers, difficulties, needs, doubts, and fears. Under her guidance, under her patronage, under her kindness and protection, nothing is to be feared; nothing is hopeless. Because, while bearing toward us a truly motherly affection and having in her care the work of our salvation, she is solicitous about the whole human race. And since she has been appointed by God to be the Queen of Heaven and earth, and is exalted above all the choirs of angels and saints, and even stands at the right hand of her only begotten Son, Jesus Christ our Lord, she presents our petitions in a most efficacious manner.

What she asks, she obtains. Her pleas can never be unheard.

Promulgation

Finally, so that this dogmatic definition pronounced by Us with regard to the Immaculate Conception of the Blessed Virgin Mary might be brought to the knowledge of the universal Church, We have wanted to record it in our present Apostolic Letters, in perpetual memory of the thing, ordering that the manuscript copies that will be made of the said Letters, or even the copies that will be printed of it, countersigned by a notary public, and bearing the seal of a person constituted in ecclesiastical dignity, might be accepted by all in absolutely the same manner as the present Letters themselves would be if they were exhibited or produced.

Therefore, no one at all may be allowed to contradict, through reckless boldness, this written text of Our declaration, decision, and definition or to attack or oppose it. If anyone has the boldness to attempt this, may he know that he will incur the wrath of the All-Powerful God and of his apostles Peter and Paul.

Given in Rome, near Saint Peter's, the eighteen hundred and fifty-fourth year of the Incarnation of Our Lord, the sixth day before the ides of December of the year 1854, the ninth of Our pontificate. 🕊

Pope Pius IX

> *She who has a Mother's heart for us was established by the Lord as Queen of heaven and earth.*

THE VIRGIN AND FRANCE

Pope Pius XI

Apostolic Letter, March 2, 1922

APOSTOLIC LETTER

Our Lady of the Assumption is proclaimed principal patroness of France, and Saint Joan of Arc, secondary patroness.

For perpetual memory

The Roman Pontiffs who were Our predecessors have always, over the course of the centuries, filled France, justly called the eldest daughter of the Church, with particular marks of their paternal affection. Our predecessor of holy memory, Pope Benedict XV, who cared deeply about the spiritual good of France, thought to give to this nation, noble above all, a special pledge of his benevolence.

In fact, when, recently, Our Venerable Brothers the cardinals, archbishops, and bishops of France, by unanimous consent, had transmitted to him by Our Venerable Brother Stanislas Touchet, bishop of Orléans, ardent and fervent supplications that he might deign to proclaim principal patroness of the French nation the Blessed Virgin Mary received into heaven and the second patroness the celestial Saint Joan, virgin of Orléans, Our predecessor thought to respond with kindness to these pious requests.

Prevented by death, he was unable to fulfill the plan he had had in mind. But for Us, who have just been raised by divine grace to the sublime Chair of the Prince of the Apostles, it is sweet and agreeable to fulfill the wish of Our very lamented Predecessor and, by Our supreme authority, to decree what could become for France a cause for good, prosperity, and happiness. It is certain, according to an old adage, that "the kingdom of France" has been called the "kingdom of Mary", and rightly so. For, from the first centuries of the Church until our time, Irenaeus and Eucherius of Lyon, Hilary of Poitiers, Anselm, who went from France to England as archbishop, Bernard of Clairvaux, Francis de Sales, and many other holy doctors, have celebrated Mary and have helped to promote and expand throughout France the cult of Virgin Mother of God. In Paris, in the very famous Sorbonne University, it has been historically proven that already in the thirteenth century the Virgin was proclaimed conceived without sin.

Even the sacred monuments give striking witness to the ancient devotion of the people to the Virgin: thirty-four cathedral churches have the title of the Virgin Mother of God, among which we like to recall as the most famous those erected in Reims, Paris, Amiens, Chartres, Coutances, and Rouen. The immense crowd of the faithful flocking from afar every year, even in our times, to the sanctuaries of Mary clearly shows how great the devotion of the people toward the Mother of God can be, and several times a year the basilica of Lourdes, as vast as it is, seems incapable of containing the innumerable crowds of pilgrims.

The Virgin Mother in person, treasurer for God of all graces, has seemed, through repeated apparitions, to approve and confirm the devotion of the French people.

Moreover, the leaders and heads of the nation have long prided themselves on affirming and defending this devotion to the Virgin. Clovis, converted to the true faith of Christ, hastened, on the ruins of a druidic temple, to lay the foundations of the Church of Notre Dame, which his son Childebert completed. Several temples were dedicated to Mary by Charlemagne. The dukes of Normandy proclaimed Mary Queen of the nation. The king Saint Louis devoutly recited the office of the Virgin every day. Louis XI, to fulfill a vow, built a temple to Our Lady in Cléry. Finally, Louis XIII dedicated the kingdom of France to Mary and ordered that every year, on the feast of the Assumption of the Virgin, some solemn offices be celebrated: and We are not unaware that these solemn celebrations continue to take place every year. In what concerns the Maid of Orléans, whom Our predecessor raised to the highest honors of the saints, no one can doubt that it was under the auspices of the Virgin that she received and fulfilled the mission of saving France. For, first of all, it was under the patronage of Our Lady of Bermont, then under that of the Virgin of Orléans, and finally of the Virgin of Reims that she undertook with a manly heart so great a work, that she remained fearless in the face of unsheathed and spotless swords in the midst of the license of the camps, that she delivered her country from supreme danger and restored the fate of France. It was after having received the counsel of her heavenly voices that she added to her glorious banner the name of Mary to that of Jesus, true King of France. Mounted on a stake, it was in whispering in the midst of the flames, in a supreme cry, the names of Jesus and Mary that she flew to heaven. Having thus experienced the obvious help of the Maid of Orléans, may France receive the favor of this second heavenly patroness: this is what was demanded by the clergy and the people, what was already agreeable to Our predecessor, and what pleases Us ourselves.

This is why, after having consulted Our Venerable Brothers, the cardinals of the Holy Roman Church in charge of the Rites, *motu proprio*, with certain knowledge and after careful deliberation, in the fullness of Our apostolic power, by the force of the present and in perpetuity, We declare and confirm that the Virgin Mary, Mother of God, under the title of her Assumption into heaven, has been properly chosen as principal patroness of all of France with God, with all the privileges and honors that belong to this noble title and this dignity.

In addition, listening to the compelling wishes of the bishops, the clergy, and the faithful of the dioceses and missions of France, We declare with the greatest joy and establish the illustrious Maid of Orléans, especially admired and venerated by all the Catholics of France as the heroine of religion and fatherland, Saint Joan of Arc, virgin, the secondary patroness of France, chosen by the full suffrage of the people and, too, according to Our supreme apostolic authority, also conceding all the honors and privileges that belong by right to this title of second patroness.

Consequently, We pray to God, author of all goods, that, through the intercession of these two heavenly patronesses, the Mother of God raised to heaven and Saint Joan of Arc, virgin, as well as other patron saints of places and titular saints of churches, as well as of dioceses and missions, Catholic France, her hopes directed toward true freedom and her ancient dignity, might be truly the firstborn daughter of the Roman Church; that she might warm up, keep, and develop through thought, action, and love her ancient and glorious traditions for the good of religion and of the fatherland.

We grant these privileges, ruling that the present Letters be and remain always firm,

valid, and effective, that they obtain and keep their full and entire effects, that they be, now and in the future, for the whole French nation, the largest pledge of heavenly help; that so they must be judged definitively and that anything that might attempt to undermine these decisions, by any authority whatsoever, knowingly or unknowingly, might be held to be in vain from now on and to have no effect for the future. Notwithstanding anything to the contrary.

Given in Rome, near Saint Peter's, under the ring of the Fisherman, March 2, of the year 1922, the first year of Our Pontificate.

Card. Gasparri, Secretary of State.

PILGRIMAGE

THE ARTICLE THAT LAUNCHED LOURDES

Louis Veuillot

L'Univers (Catholic Union), appeared August 28, 1858

France
Paris, August 27,

THE LOURDES GROTTO

Lourdes is a small town in the High Pyrenees, very old, more passed through than known. It sits on the first steps of a mountain staircase, at the edge of the road from Tarbes to Pau, between Bagnères and the shrine renamed Betharam. It is crossed in order to go from Bagnères to Cauterets. The traveler who looks over these valleys, full of magnificent and charming spectacles, notes the old and picturesque fortified castle of Lourdes, the garrison, successively, of the Romans, the Saracens, who, it is said, wanted only to return it to Notre-Dame-du-Puy, the English, who kept it for a long time; an object of desire often disputed in civil wars, the cradle of legends, theatre of fighting and suffering, today peacefully guarded by an infantry platoon. At the foot of this castle, built on rock, the roaring Gave passes. Very close by, on the edge of the torrent, is the grotto, inconspicuous and, until now, very rarely visited, where, for several months, the testimony of a little poor girl has been attracting so many curious people.

The village is not at all sleepy and deprived of what is called today the "lights". It is the seat of a lower court; there are large houses, fine inns, cafés, a circle well-supplied with newspapers. Travelers, although they stop briefly at Lourdes, do not let current ideas be thrown out there, or sometimes even those that are not current: they find those to whom they should speak, we have proof of that. Lourdes has a journal, *Le Lavedan, journal de l'arrondissement d'Argelès* [*Le Lavedan*, paper for the borough of Argelès], which is moderate, but ill-disposed to believe anything that is not attested to by the police commissioner and authorized by the subprefect. The population is lively, intelligent, still Christian on the whole, more advanced in its luminaries, dispassionate, let us hasten to say, and generally without the kind of bias that closes its eyes to evidence based on facts or reason. A month ago, on the doorstep of a café, while waiting for the coach, with everyone being preoccupied with supernatural events, we had the occasion to attend and take part in a discussion where these matters were debated. Certainly, the very diverse opinions would not have been different in most Parisian meetings, even if carried on in better language. And we would be happy if the press would often show the

same good faith, openness of spirit, and the perfect courtesy with which the speakers allow a stranger to give them his opinion and, at certain moments, contradict them.

It was here that we began to study the reputedly amazing facts of Lourdes. We had not paid great attention to what the newspapers were saying about it, and they were nearly unknown to us. Here they are in all simplicity.

On the past February 11, a little fourteen-year-old girl named Bernadette, belonging to one of the poorest families, very ignorant and not having made her First Communion yet, had been sent by her parents into the woods at the gates of the city to gather some dry branches. Some children of her age accompanied her,

doing the same job. It was necessary to cross a current of water. Bernadette's companions passed over, crying out that the water was cold; she hesitated and was the last to stay. Facing her, on the other side of the stream, was the rock that was to become so famous. There are three excavations to be noted there: one at the bottom, to the left; the second in the middle, rather like a window, and adorned with brambles and other flowering plants; the third, above, a little to the right. The weather was calm. Bernadette, having finally decided to go across the water, began to take her shoes off, when she suddenly heard a noise like a gust of wind. She raised her eyes, saw nothing, and thought she had been mistaken. The noise was repeated, and she

ROCK

looked again; while the surrounding trees remained motionless, the small branches that were next to the grotto in the middle seemed agitated by a current of air. Almost immediately, a lady dressed in white appeared at this opening and made a sign to the young girl to come. Bernadette called to her companions: "Look, look", she cried to them, "that lady, at the entrance to the grotto!" The children looked and thought that Bernadette was joking. She herself thought that it was an illusion, rubbed her eyes, and asked the others if they really saw nothing. But the vision was still there, smiling and making a sign for her to come. Bernadette hesitated no more, went across the stream, and knelt in front of the grotto, her rosary in her hand. The other children, angry with her, came to pick her up and make her return to the town. In the evening, her parents noted her preoccupation and wanted to know the cause of it. She told them what she thought she had seen. They tried, though in vain, to dissuade her.

It was Thursday. The following Sunday, Quinquagesima Sunday, Bernadette, accompanied by her companions, returned to the grotto. She had the same vision there, and again the following Thursday, February 18. An irresistible attraction had brought her back this third time. That day, she said, the lady spoke to her, recommending that she come to the grotto every morning for fifteen consecutive days. The child began this pilgrimage the next day.

Few people accompanied her the first two days; on the third, Sunday, February 21, as the public began to take a lot of interest in this adventure, the police feared some kind of deception and some disturbance. They had her called in and subjected her to a long interrogation. The child's answers seemed simple, precise, natural, and without any contradiction. She gave an account of all the circumstances of the apparition and described in detail the figure she had seen, her demeanor, her height, her dress, her usual attitude. Both threats and caresses were used to make her err and contradict herself; she repeated her account and maintained it. If someone summarized this narration, intentionally introducing some variant, she observed that this was not what she had said.

Everyone attests to this. Yet, whatever explanation is given for the facts recounted by the young girl, and there are all kinds of them, no one up to the present has suspected her good faith; and the respectable priest of Lourdes, whose prudence has been praised by all, admitted her to First Communion. We have seen and heard Bernadette. She is small for her age, although in good health; she has an intelligent appearance, not at all cunning, beautiful eyes; she speaks without boldness and without timidity. Not wishing to embarrass her (other people have attempted very skillfully to do that, but without success), yet, due to certain circumstances, we asked her if she had heard of the children of La Salette. She had heard of them after the vision. "If you are lying, do you know how guilty you will be?" Someone had already said that to her. "And what do you plan to do? Don't you think that some charitable people will one day take care of you?" She smiled, looking at her poor clothing. Several times she has been offered money or objects that might tempt her. She has consistently refused everything, and her disinterestedness is no more in doubt than her sincerity. The *Lady* has promised her that she would be happy, but not in this life.

Let's go over the rest of the facts again. The local authority requested Bernadette's father to prevent her from going to the grotto; he seemed quite willing and promised to do so. The child, after having received the prohibition and being resolved to obey, she said, did not obey. She went to the grotto by a roundabout path, claiming that an inner force was doing violence to her. They no longer tried to restrain her.

The scene in front of the grotto was curious and moving. Every morning, there were more than a thousand people who returned, crying out about the miracle. And what had they seen? Absolutely nothing except the child on her knees in prayer. That was the whole object of their admiration and the whole foundation of their faith, which was, moreover, full and profound. We have questioned several witnesses of this spectacle. It had already stopped for nearly five months; it was subject to all the disputes, all the ridicule, and their impression remained serious and lively.

"I went for the first time on February 24th", one of these witnesses told us, "prepared to examine closely and, to be honest, to be much amused, expecting only a comedy. At the usual time, seven o'clock in the morning, Bernadette appeared; I was close to her. She knelt down naturally, without constraint and without any trouble, drew out her rosary and began to pray. Soon her gaze, which had become more animated and, to put it better, completely transformed, was fixed on the opening of the rock. I myself saw only the stripped branches of the shrub, and yet what will I tell you? I remained convinced that a mysterious being was standing there. Bernadette no longer had the same face, another mind was painted there; her least

She opened her large eyes, insatiable to see.

gestures, the way in which she made the sign of the cross, had a surprising nobility; in the end, she was another person. She opened her large eyes, insatiable to see; she was afraid to lower her eyelids and lose sight of the wonder she was contemplating; she was smiling at this invisible wonder, and all of this gave the idea of ecstasy and bliss. I was no less moved than the other spectators. Like them, I held my breath in order to try to hear the conversation that seemed to be established between the vision and the child. The latter was listening with the expression of the most profound respect; sometimes a shade of sadness passed over her face, but the usual expression was that of great joy. I observed that at certain moments she was not breathing. During all this time, she had her rosary in her hand, sometimes motionless, sometimes passing irregularly between her fingers or making the usual movement, all perfectly in relation to the look on her face, which expressed in turn admiration, prayer, joy. At intervals, she made those very pious and noble signs of the cross of which I've spoken to you.

"The rosary finished, Bernadette dragged herself on her knees from the point where she was praying to the entrance of the grotto; it was a distance of about fifty feet. At certain times, on the order she said she had received, she went to drink from the water that comes out of the rock, on the left. After a prayer under the rock, where she still saw the Lady, she said, she returned to the starting point and began her rosary once more. Her face was illuminated again, and we saw the first scene renewed. The child entered into this state, and she left it smoothly, through a transition so very gradual that the precise moment of transformation could not be detected. She would get up and return to the city path again in the midst of the crowd. She was a poor little girl in rags who seemed only to have taken the common part in this surprising spectacle."

The same witness made several visits to the grotto; he always saw the same thing, only each time he saw a larger crowd. That crowd was calm. Most were praying with a rosary in their hand; no one showed any signs of disrespect. Even those who, without making any accusation of deception, believed it to be an illusion, respected its character and removed their hats.

Two days before the end of the fortnight set by the vision, Bernadette went to find the curé of Lourdes and told him that the Lady of the grotto was asking for a chapel at the site of the apparition. Monsieur le Curé, who had, like all the clergy, kept away, observing the facts, replied that it was first of all necessary to know who this lady was. Bernadette returned to the grotto on March 25, the feast of the Annunciation, and begged the Lady to tell her her name. To three repeated requests, the vision replied only with a smile; then, finally, still smiling, she said that she was Mary Immaculate, or, rather, to use Bernadette's very expression, the Immaculate Conception. She instructed the child to renew the request for the chapel. On

"" *Her face was illuminated again.* ""

people had visited it, and without noticing anything there because, in fact, there was nothing extraordinary there. It seems, however, that the soil was wet and that there was a kind of oozing, but that it was nearly imperceptible. The first time Bernadette wanted to drink, she brought back in her hands and lifted to her lips only a kind of mud. Today, the fountain provides a pure and fairly abundant water.

Everyone wanted to drink that water. A great number of sick and infirm people claimed to have found an almost sudden cure there; and in fact, cases of very strange cures that seem incontestable have been cited; several have been confirmed by doctors and by other entirely trustworthy people. At the moment, some of the alleged facts appear so self-evident that one would not think of questioning them; the skeptics are content to explain them by the very powerful mineral properties that must be possessed by the water of Massabielle, which is the name of the grotto.

These same people, not wanting to question the sincerity of the child, had said that she was cataleptic.

Science, up to now, has not confirmed these scientific explanations. The child enjoys very good physical and moral health, and the water, analyzed by a famous chemist from Toulouse, is, in his opinion, quite simply pure water. Then they began to deny the cures, since the water, by its own properties, could not have worked them. But there are observations, documents, and living witnesses against which this negation cannot prevail.

Let us now turn to facts of another order and see the different interventions of civil authority and of religious authority.

The rumors about the wonders that were taking place at Lourdes, magnified by the fame, as one can imagine, had drawn to the grotto a large number of pilgrims and curious people. They numbered several thousand at a time; the total number of them is incalculable. There was,

that same day, she announced that Bernadette would not be happy on earth, but happiness was awaiting her in heaven.

Bernadette added one detail that should be noted: the vision told her three things that she was not to reveal and that concerned her exclusively. Several people had a bad opinion of this circumstance and of this mystery. The little girl was told this. She did not defend herself and persevered in this as in the rest.

Such are the stories of Bernadette. One important factor has not helped much to substantiate them. We have spoken of water that springs from the rock at the place where, on orders she received from the vision, the child sometimes drank during the intervals between her ecstasies. There are great disputes of several kinds about this water.

First of all, according to some, the fountain was flowing before the apparition; according to others, it has flowed only since then. The grotto was largely unknown, and only a few however, no material disorder, and the police did not publicly specify any. Pilgrims and the curious came, some to pray, others to watch; they drank water at the fountain, and withdrew politely, as they had come. The priests in the vicinity had more penitents at confession; that was the only harm. Yet, while the religious authority observed in silence and did not complain, the civil authority, which had no reprehensible event to combat and which was not charged with preventing citizens from going either to pray or to watch peacefully where good seemed to them to be, found that these manifestations were upsetting order and could destroy religion. Without consulting the religious authority, which was asking nothing of them, they set out not only to reestablish order but to protect religion.

Pious hands had built in front of the rock a kind of small oratory: a few candles, a few flowers, a few images; a few offerings for the construction of the future chapel were placed there. That was found to be contrary to a law; and, on May 4, the day when the prefect of Hautes-Pyrénées was in Lourdes to hold the review board, all these objects, including the offerings, were removed on his order. This measure satisfied a certain number of local philosophers, far from being the majority in the land, but who were only more impatient and irritated by the gathering that was forming around the grotto and by all the consequences that they saw there. The semi-official newspapers reported this removal as a great and salutary victory. We would not be sorry to listen to them; there is a tone of administrative piety.

"For some time, the scenes that had taken place at the Lourdes grotto had taken on the character of a kind that attracted the attention of the authorities.

"Contrary to the requirements of the law, the grotto had been decorated with religious emblems and thus transformed, *without authorization*, into a kind of oratory where candles burned night and day. The most absurd rumors circulated about alleged miracles that had taken place; new visionaries were revealed at every moment[1] and *all true friends of religion were dismayed by this state of affairs.*

"Last Tuesday, the day of the revisions at Lourdes, the prefect, taking advantage of the presence of all the mayors of the canton, who were meeting on this occasion, showed them how regrettable the scenes that had been produced were and *what disfavor they tended to cast on religion*. He applied himself *particularly* to making them understand that the act of creating an oratory at the grotto, an act *sufficiently*

---

1. Two or three children, for reasons that remain unknown, also claimed to have had visions. They were dismissed from catechism class, and that was it.

constituted by the deposit of religious emblems and candles, was an attack made on the ecclesiastical authority as well as the civil authority; an illegality that it was the administration's duty to stop, since, in terms of the law, any public chapel or oratory could not be founded without the authorization of the Government, on the advice of the diocesan bishop.

"The prefect added that his feelings should not appear suspicious to anyone, that everyone in the department knew his profound respect for religion and that he believed he had given enough proof for it not to be possible to misinterpret his intentions. In concluding, he let it be known that he had just given the order to the police commissioner to remove and transport to the town hall, where they would be available to those who had deposited them, the objects placed in the grotto; *that he had, in addition, issued instructions that the persons who said they were visionaries were to be arrested and taken to Tarbes in order to be treated as sick persons, at the expense of the department, and that he would pursue as spreaders of false news all those who contributed to spreading the absurd rumors that had been circulating.*

"These words were greeted by unanimous enthusiasm. As for the instructions issued by the prefect, they were carried out by the police commissioner alone and accomplished without the least opposition on the part of the inhabitants of Lourdes. It would be impossible to congratulate ourselves too much about this result, which all sane men had been desiring for a long time. There is reason to hope now that the common sense of the people and the wise intervention of the clergy, who better than anyone can guide and enlighten them, will do the

rest."—Septavaux (from the Tarbes newspaper *Ère impériale*).

Le Lavedan, a Lourdes newspaper, got hold of this strong piece. And as *Intérêt public*, another Tarbes newspaper, had dared to express less admiration for the prefectorial measure, *Le Lavedan* wondered if one wanted to "censure the wise measures taken by the administration superior in order to put an end to the stupid masquerades and to a *shameful exploitation of the people's credulity*." We can see that the religious zeal of the editor of the *Lavedan* does not prevent him from using lively words. Alas! If we were in charge of the government, how could we restrain all those Christians?

Yet, despite the *unanimous enthusiasm* of the mayors, everything did not turn out according to the predictions of the *Ère impériale* and the desires of the *Lavedan*. The people were in truth very calm, calmer than it was perhaps wise to hope of a people strongly attached to their beliefs and who in many circumstances showed

> *The people were in truth very calm, calmer than it was perhaps wise to hope.*

that it was necessary to respect even their superstitions.[2] They allowed the police commissioner alone to remove the religious objects deposited close to the grotto; but they replaced them with others, and continuing to come every night to the grotto, they sang the litanies. These are the stupid masquerades of which the elegant editor of the *Lavedan* was speaking.

They then had recourse to other means. On June 8, 1848, the mayor of Lourdes, "**in view of the instructions** addressed to him by the superior authority" and various laws of 1789, 1790, 1793, and 1827, on municipal administration:

- Considering that it is important, in the interest of religion, to put an end to the regrettable scenes that are taking place at the Massabielle grotto, located in Lourdes, on the left bank of the Gave;
- Considering, on the other hand, that the duty of the mayor is to ensure local public health;
- Considering that the large number of its citizens and of people from outside the municipality come to draw water from a spring in that grotto;
- Considering that there are serious reasons to think that this water contains mineral elements and that it is prudent, before allowing usage, to wait for a scientific analysis to make known the applications that could be made of it by medicine; that, in addition, the law submits the use of mineral springs to the prior authorization of the Government;

Stop:

- Art. 1. It is forbidden to take water from the aforesaid spring.
- Art. 2. It is also forbidden to pass over the communal side of said shore of Massabielle.
- Art. 3. There will be set up at the entrance of the grotto a barrier to prevent access to it. Posts will also be placed there bearing these words: *It is forbidden to enter this property*.
- Art. 4. Any violation of the present decree will be prosecuted in accordance with the law.
- Art. 5. The police commissioner, the police, the rural police force, and the municipal authorities remain in charge of executing this decree.

This decree, like the previous measures of the prefect, show clearly what practical freedom has become in France under the care of political freedom![3] It was implemented. They surrounded the grotto, at the bottom of the rock, with a barrier of boards; a pole was erected at the entrance to the path; they reported the decree to the people of the country who persisted in coming to these forbidden places and in drawing water from the fountain—which they did not, however, prevent from flowing, undoubtedly because it was still reputed to be mineral water. The reporting was followed by

---

2. Among the other facts reported by Bascle de Lagrèze in his interesting *Chronique de la ville et du château de Lourdes* (Chronicle of the town and castle of Lourdes), we will quote this one:

"The people are convinced that the foreigner who happens to die accidentally outside his country must be buried in the township where he breathed his last breath and that the township that failed in this duty of hospitality would be punished within a year by some terrible scourge. Several years ago, after a young man from the Azun valley died in the Lourdes lake, his family asked for the body again. They could not obtain it. The whole population of Lourdes, ordinarily so peaceful, rose up. The voice of the magistrates was ignored, and their courage nearly became disastrous. A collision became inevitable. The family withdrew, lest the coffin be stained with blood. The people calmed down only after being assured that the body was truly lying in the grave and that they were not being duped by some mock burial."

3. See, for Lourdes in particular, the work that we have just cited. The author, analyzing the jurisdictions and privileges of the town of Lourdes in the Middle Ages, makes this remark: "We cannot without astonishment consider what high degree of freedom our fathers achieved during the feudal period and how many generous ideas, believed to be the daughters of the Revolution, had preceded it by more than six centuries." And these were not only *ideas*.

convictions with a five-franc fine, jointly and severally. At the same time, although Bernadette was not stopped in order to have her cared for at the hospice, it was proved that the prefect had not spoken in vain. Three women were sued in the civil court of Lourdes, accused of reproducing false news likely to disturb the public peace. They had said that an order had come from Paris to replace the objects taken from the grotto and that the emperor was asking Bernadette to pray for him. Two of these women were released, the third fined. On appeal, the imperial court of Pau dismissed the complaint against all three of them. As for the convictions pronounced by the justice of the peace for infractions of the municipal regulations, we do not know what resulted from those. It also appears that only people from this country were reported, not foreigners. We know people who have visited the grotto and drawn water since the prohibition without being bothered in any way. These persons saw on dry places, in the middle of the Gave bed, in front of the grotto, children, women, and poor people on their knees, who had come there across the water in order to avoid the forbidden path and to satisfy their piety without risking having to pay the fine. Often, it is said, even the agents the municipal authority has placed on guard at its post, before beginning their shift, go down to the grotto, kneel, and make their prayer.

So, although the gathering has been greatly diminished, the harsh measures of the authority have not produced any moral effect; rather, they have even provoked the feeling the authority wanted to overcome; and finally, since it is not possible to enforce the measures strictly, many infractions are tolerated and remain unpunished. An unfortunate example. The religious authority, whose adherence to these administrative measures has been alleged without cause, one might say inappropriately, has acted very differently. This will be seen by means of the episcopal document that we are going to

reproduce. That authority waited, it examined, it allowed time for the facts and the dissent to be produced and for the emotions and passions to calm down. In taking up the cause, it prejudged nothing. It announced an examination that would, this time, be completely in depth and decisive, at least insofar as the decision that it may have to give. This examination will be done slowly, in all possible conditions of light, fairness, and freedom, with respect for the intelligence and the conscience of the people.

We have reported the events as they happened, or at least such as the public voice recounts them, trying at keep at a distance from the emotions by which they are still animated and the affirmations that they produce. All that remains is for us to listen to the venerable bishop of Tarbes and to wait for the results of the instruction that he has ordered. May we be permitted, however, one observation.

It seems to us that what has just happened at Lourdes throws an interesting light on the general origin of pilgrimages. One almost always finds there, at the beginning, events similar to those that are concerning us. It is an apparition, a revelation, an image that has been found, an unexpected grace, attested by popular faith, contested sometimes by the learned, sometimes by the wise, or those who think they are. The popular faith persists in spite of everything. The Church intervenes. It is without doubt undeniable that she has the right and duty to intervene: she owes the truth to God and to the people. Who will pronounce it if not she? Who is a better judge of the importance of the events? Who will better verify the miracle? Who will better sort out the illusion, better unmask and reverse deception and error? Let us recall that alleged miracle worker who for several days, seven or eight years ago, made such a loud noise in a city of the Avignon diocese. There, contrary to what is happening in Lourdes, the supernatural was admitted and attested to by the agents of the civil authority.

The reports of the gendarmerie and those of the subprefect concluded in favor of the miracle. The first examination by the archbishop was enough to expose the deception, and the alleged miracle worker had no more supporters. But if the Church, having examined the facts, recognizes the work of God, no further denial prevails, and the pilgrimage is founded; the torrent of prayer is carried to these chosen places with a vigor that the centuries have not weakened. Interrupted at times, it resumes, as

we see in our day, as full and irresistible as in the past. Thus, the La Salette pilgrimage has been established through incomparable contradictions. Thus will be established, if the Church permits, the Lourdes pilgrimage, whatever one wants to do to stop it.

And why would one stop it in the case where the instruction ordered by the competent authority establishes that it has pleased God to let fall there, through the Holy Virgin, those graces that he distributes to whatever places and on whatever people he pleases? The prefect of the Hautes-Pyrénées held the review board when he removed from the grotto the small objects and humble offerings that the faithful had deposited there. He was responsible, that day, for imposing on his citizens a rather large, rather heavy duty, and one initiated in a rather disgusting way: he could have understood, if he had wanted to, that some consoling freedoms are necessary as compensation for the sacrifices demanded by society. Now the freedom to pray in certain places, to burn a candle, to draw a drop of water there, even to deposit an offering there cannot seem very burdensome to the State or disastrous to public order or offensive to personal modesty and freedom: yet it profoundly consoles those who use it. These are "stupid masquerades", says the editor of *Lavedan*. Perhaps the editor of *Lavedan* was not well informed. In any case, in the vast collection of our laws, we doubt that there is one that obliges the majority of the inhabitants of Lourdes and of the Argelès district to regulate their religious beliefs and practices according to the refined taste of the editor of *Lavedan*. Nor do we believe that it would be a wise policy either to use such language or to regulate the administration according to the feelings that inspire it. The faith of the last shepherd of the Pyrenees is worth more than all of that spirit, deserves more consideration, profits society more. The faith of these shepherds serves to make honest people, good soldiers, good fathers of families, good taxpayers, if one limits to such work the wishes of the administration. We do not deny that something could be done with the spirit of the editor of *Lavedan*, but certainly nothing preferable to these sure results of faith. Recently, at Tarbes, there had been only a single case, and a very slight one, about the role of foundations; the session was emptied in an instant. The learned magistrate who was presiding congratulated the country on this scarcity of crimes: he attributed it to the influence of the jubilee that had just been celebrated in the diocese and in no way to the reading of the *Ère impériale* and *Lavedan*. At Lourdes, the parish priest told us, the grotto has been the true and only preacher of the jubilee, which was the richest in fruits of penance and in returns to God. So let the faith live! In your jobs, in your powers, in your fortunes, consider that most of the men you govern need to ask God for bread every day and receive it every day only through a kind of miracle. Faith is already bread. It helps the eating of black bread; it helps in waiting again patiently, past the hour when it was supposed to come. And when God seems to want to open one of these places of grace where faith flows more abundantly and gives quicker help, do not close it; you yourselves, the first ones, will have need of it. It is there that you will be able to cut some costs in the budget of hospitals and prisons. 🐦

Louis Veuillot

66 *Without constraint and without any trouble, she drew out her rosary and began to pray.* 99

DECREE OF BISHOP LAURENCE

Fathers Sempé and Duboé

January 18, 1862

Finally, on January 18, 1862, the *Decree of His Excellency, the Bishop of Tarbes, concerning the reality of the apparition at the Grotto of Lourdes appeared.*

Bishop Laurence, in a few lines, established, first of all, the fact of divine apparitions under both Testaments, pointed out the apparitions of the Holy Virgin Mary in the history of the Church, and reported, in substance, the account of the apparition at the Grotto. Then, presenting the necessity of slow studies for the appreciation of superhuman events, he developed in a full, luminous, and unassailable discussion the reasons for his judgment.

Dearly beloved brethren; the event of which we are speaking has been, for the past four years, the object of our solicitude; we have followed it in its various phases; we have kept ourselves informed of the findings of the commission composed of pious, learned, and experienced priests who have questioned the child, studied the facts, examined, and weighed everything. We have also called in men of science, and we have remained convinced that the apparition is supernatural and divine and that consequently what Bernadette saw is the Blessed Virgin. Our conviction is based on the testimony of Bernadette but more especially on the other facts which have taken place and which cannot be explained except by divine intervention.

The testimony of the young girl presents all the guarantees we could ask for. First of all, her sincerity cannot be called into question. Who does not admire, in being near her, the simplicity, the candor, and the modesty of this child? While the rest of the world speaks of the wondrous things that have been revealed to her, she alone of all keeps silence; she speaks only when she is questioned; then she relates everything with a touching sincerity and without any affectation of any kind. To the numerous questions that are put to her she gives, without any hesitation, clear, precise answers, answers

Translation of the decree taken from "Decree of His Excellency, the Bishop of Tarbes", Lourdes Documents of Bishop Laurence, Bishop of Tarbes, 1845–1870, no. 61, pp. 5–14, on the Internet at: https://ecommons.udayton.edu/cgi/viewcontent.cgi?article=1060&context=marian _reprints.

that are to the point and are characterized by a strong conviction. In spite of having to undergo severe trials, she has never been shaken by any threats; she has answered the most generous offers with the noblest disinterestedness. Without once contradicting herself in the different questionings to which she has been subjected, she has constantly maintained what she has said without adding or retracting anything. Bernadette's sincerity, then, is undeniable. Let us add that it has not been challenged. Even those who have contradicted her—and there were some—have had to render this testimony themselves.

But if Bernadette did not wish to deceive anyone, was she herself not deceived? Did she not believe that she saw and heard what she actually did not see or hear? Was she not the victim of a hallucination? How could we believe this? The wisdom of her answers reveals in this child an upright spirit, a calm imagination, and good sense beyond her age. Religious sentiment never went to extremes in her; no one has ever dared to say that in the girl there was ever any intellectual disorder, aberration of the senses, oddity of character, nor morbid affections which might have disposed her to creations of the imagination. She saw the apparition not once but eighteen times; at first she saw it quite unexpectedly and suddenly when there was nothing that could have prepared her for this happening; then during the two weeks when she expected to see the Lady every day, she saw nothing on two days although she was in the same place and under identical circumstances. And then, what happened during the apparitions? A transformation took place in Bernadette: her countenance took on a new expression, there was a special sparkle in her eyes, she saw things she would never again see and heard words she would never again hear. In fact, she did not always understand their meaning, but she would always retain the memory of them. These circumstances put together do

not permit us to believe in hallucination; the young girl had really seen a being calling herself the Immaculate Conception. Since this phenomenon cannot be explained naturally, we are forced to the conclusion that the apparition is supernatural.

The testimony of Bernadette, important as it is by itself, takes on added strength, we should even say, finds its complement in the wonderful things that have taken place since the first occurrence. If we must judge a tree by its fruits, then we can say that the apparition as described by the young girl is supernatural and divine for it has produced supernatural and divine effects. What has happened, dearly beloved brethren? Scarcely had the apparition become known when the news spread like wildfire. People knew that Bernadette was to go to the Grotto for a period of two weeks: the whole region is stirred up, crowds hasten to the place of the apparition; with religious impatience they await the solemn moment; while the girl

in ecstasy is lost in the object of her contemplation, the witnesses of this wonder are touched with emotion as they share in the same sentiments of wonderment and prayer.

The apparitions have ceased, but people continue to come in crowds: pilgrims from distant regions as well as from the neighborhood hasten to the Grotto; here we see people of all ages, classes of society, and conditions. What is the impelling force that draws these many visitors? They come to the Grotto to pray and ask favors of Mary Immaculate. By their recollected bearing, they attest to the fact that they are experiencing, as it were, a divine breath which animates these rocks that have become so famous. Souls that are already Christian find themselves strengthened in virtue; men affected by indifference are brought back to the practice of their religion; obstinate sinners are once more reconciled to God in answer to prayers addressed to Our Lady of Lourdes on their behalf. These marvels of grace, which have a universal and lasting character, can only have God as their sole Author: Do they not, in consequence, confirm the reality of the apparition?

If, from the effects produced for the good of souls, we pass over to those which concern the health of the body, what new wonders do we not have to relate? We have seen Bernadette drink and wash her face in the spot pointed out by the apparition; this circumstance had aroused public attention. People asked themselves if this was not an indication of a super-

> ## "The sick tried the waters of the Grotto and not without success."

natural virtue that had descended upon the spring at Massabielle. With this thought in mind, the sick tried the waters of the Grotto and not without success. A number of those whose diseases had resisted every treatment, even the most energetic, suddenly recovered their health. These extraordinary cures had a terrific repercussion; the news spread far and near. Sick from all countries asked for the water from Massabielle when they themselves could not come to the Grotto. How many sick were cured, how many families consoled!… If we should wish to call for their testimony, innumerable voices would be raised, with the note of gratitude, to proclaim the supreme efficacy of the water of the Grotto. We cannot here enumerate all the favors received, but what we ought to tell you is that the water of Massabielle has cured sick who had been given up and declared incurable. These cures have taken place with the use of water which lacks any natural curative quality according

to the reports of expert chemists who have made a rigorous analysis of it. These cures have occurred, some suddenly, others after the application of this water two or three times, whether in the form of a drink or as a lotion. Besides, these cures are permanent. What is the power that has produced them? Is it a force in the organism? Science, which has been consulted on the subject, answers in the negative. Therefore, these cures are the work of God. They are related to the apparition; this is their point of departure; this has inspired the confidence of the sick. There is then a close connection between the cures and the apparition; the apparition is divine since the cures carry the mark of the divine in them. But what comes from God is truth! Consequently, the apparition calling herself the Immaculate Conception, whom Bernadette saw and heard, is the Most Holy Virgin Mary! Let us then cry out: the finger of God is here! *Digitus Dei est hic.*

How can we fail to admire, dearly beloved brethren, the economy of Divine Providence? Toward the end of 1854, the immortal Pius IX proclaimed the dogma of the Immaculate Conception. The echoes carried the words of the Pontiff to the ends of the earth; the hearts of Catholics beat with joy and everywhere the glorious privilege of Mary was celebrated by feasts the memory of which will remain forever engraved in our memories. And behold, just about three years later, the holy Virgin, appearing to a child, says to her: *I am the Immaculate Conception.… I desire that a chapel be built here in my honor.* Does she not seem to want to consecrate by a special monument the infallible voice of the successor of Saint Peter? Where does she wish this monument built? Right at the foot of our own Pyrenees Mountains where numerous foreigners come from all parts of the world to seek health in our hot springs. Might we not say that she invites the faithful of all nations to come and

honor her in the new shrine that will be built to her?

Be glad, you citizens of Lourdes! The august Virgin Mary deigns to cast her looks of mercy upon you. She wishes that, next to your city, there be built a sanctuary where she will spread her favors. Thank her for this evidence of predilection she gives you; since she showers upon you all the tendernesses of a mother, show yourselves her devoted children by the imitation of her virtues and your unshakable attachment to your holy faith.

Moreover, we are pleased to recognize that the apparition has already borne the fruits of salvation among you. Eye witnesses as you have been of the happenings at the Grotto and of their blessed results, your confidence has been as great as your conviction has been strong. We have admired your prudence and your docility in following the counsels of submission to civil authority when for several weeks you had to stop your visits to the Grotto; then you had to stem the tide of the sentiments in your hearts, sentiments inspired by the spectacle which you beheld with your own eyes during the two weeks of the apparitions. And you, dearly beloved faithful of our diocese, open your hearts to hope: a new era of grace is beginning for you; you are all called upon to gather your share of the blessings promised to us. In your supplications, in your hymns, you will henceforth mingle the name of Our Lady of Lourdes with the blessed names of Our Lady of Garaison, of Poeylaün, of Héas, of Piétat.

From the heights of these holy sanctuaries, the Immaculate Virgin will watch over you and will shield you with her protection. Yes, my beloved brethren, if, with the heart full of confidence, we keep our eyes fixed on this Star of the Sea, we shall withstand, without fear of shipwreck, the tempests of life and shall arrive safe and sound in the harbor of eternal happiness.

FOR THESE REASONS

After having conferred with our venerable brothers the dignitaries, the canons, and the chapter of our cathedral church:

AFTER HAVING INVOKED THE NAME OF GOD,

Basing ourselves on the rules wisely laid down by Benedict XIV in his book on the beatification and canonization of saints for distinguishing between true and false visions;

Considering the favorable report presented to us by the commission charged with examining the apparition at the Grotto of Lourdes and the facts accompanying it;

Considering the written testimony of medical doctors whom we have consulted on the numerous cures following the use of the water at the Grotto;

Considering the fact of the apparition both from the standpoint of the girl who has testified concerning it and more especially from the extraordinary effects produced so that it cannot be explained except by the intervention of a supernatural cause;

Considering that this cause can only be divine since the effects produced being, on the one hand, sensible signs of grace such as the conversion of sinners, and on the other hand, deviations from the laws of nature such as the miraculous cures, can only be referred to the Author of grace and the Lord of all nature;

Considering, finally, that our conviction is strengthened by the mighty spontaneous concourse of the faithful at the Grotto, a concourse which has not ceased since the first apparitions and the purpose of which is to beg favors or to give thanks for those already received;

In order to respond to the legitimate impatience of our venerable chapter, of the clergy and laity of our diocese, and of so many pious souls who, for a long lime, have requested a decision from ecclesiastical authority, a decision which motives of prudence caused us to delay;

Wishing also to satisfy the desire of several of our colleagues in the episcopacy and of a great number of distinguished persons outside the diocese;

After having invoked the light of the Holy Spirit and the assistance of the Most Holy Virgin,

WE HAVE DECLARED AND DO DECLARE AS FOLLOWS:

Article 1. We judge that the Immaculate Mary, Mother of God, really appeared lo Bernadette Soubirous on February 11, 1858, and following days, eighteen times in the Grotto of Massabielle, near the city of Lourdes; that this Apparition possesses all the characteristics of truth and that the faithful may believe in it with certainty.

We humbly submit our judgment to that of the Sovereign Pontiff to whom is committed the government of the universal Church.

Art. 2. We authorize the cult of Our Lady of the Grotto of Lourdes in our diocese but we forbid the publication of any special prayers, hymns, or books of devotion relating to this event without our written approval.

Art. 3. In order to accede to the request of the Blessed Virgin expressed several times during the apparitions, we propose to construct a sanctuary on the terrain of the Grotto which has become the property of the Bishop of Tarbes.

In view of the rugged and difficult nature of the site, this construction will call for much work and for relatively considerable funds. 🕊

HYMN

Joseph Roumanille

On music by Nicolas Saboly,

Collection published by Adolphe Dargien, organist at Lourdes, 1875

Nostro-Damo, à Massabielo,
D'en Prouvenço sian vengu:
A la Miraclouso pielo
En pregant aven bégu …

O Mario ! La patrio,
L'aubouraras;
Sout ti bras
L'assoustaras,
Et la counsoularas.

Nostro-Damo d'Esperanço,
A ti pèd sian à geinoun:
Pèr lou salut de la Franço
Venèn invouca toun noum.

O Mario ! La patrio,
L'aubouraras;
Sout ti bras
L'assoustaras,
Et la counsoularas.

Nostro-Damo de Refuge,
L'Infernau nous agarris:
Autant-lèu lou veirein fuge,
Se ta gràci nous sourris.

O Mario! La patrio,
L'aubouraras;
Sout ti bras
L'assoustaras,
Et la counsoularas.

Nostro-Damo de Vitòri,
Nous abandounes jamai;
Sousto-nous, Tourre d'evòri,
Vuei, deman e longo-mai!

O Mario! La patrio,
L'aubouraras;
Sout ti bras
L'assoustaras,
Et la counsoularas.

Nostro-Damo Immaculado,
Ile blanc di Pirenèu
De la Franço desoulado
Fai resplendi lou drapèu.

O Mario! La patrio,
L'aubouraras;
Sout ti bras
L'assoustaras,
Et la counsoularas.

Nostro-Damo di Miracle,
Mete en pas pichots e grand,
Et Diéu te fague l'ouracle
Di tèms urous que vendran!

O Mario! La patrio,
L'aubouraras;
Sout ti bras
L'assoustaras,
Et la counsoularas.

Nostro-Damo de la Grâci,
Gardo-nous de mancamen!
Et pièi, pourquen, fàci à fàci
Véire Diéu eternamen!

O Mario! La patrio,
L'aubouraras;
Sout ti bras
L'assoustaras,
Et la counsoularas.

"*The pilgrimage ticket has a true value, of which the management must give an exact accounting to the Companies.*"

THE DEPARTURE

Anonymous

Reims manual for the pilgrimage to Lourdes

Departure ceremony

On the day before the departure, or the same day, in the morning, the solemn ceremony called the departure ceremony is celebrated at the cathedral or in any other designated church.

Singing of the *Magnificat*.

Special address and advice to pilgrims.—Benediction of the Most Blessed Sacrament.

Then, blessing of the pilgrimage badges.

To close, singing of the Lourdes *Ave Maria*.

The badges thus blessed the day before are distributed in the compartments to each of the pilgrims ten minutes before departure.

All are asked not to wear any external sign, cross, or patient card before the departure from Reims.

Departure

It is necessary for the sick to be at the station half an hour, and the non-disabled at least twenty minutes, before the scheduled time of departure.

Tickets

Each pilgrim will carry:

1. A name card proving that he belongs to the pilgrimage. This card is yellow in third class, green in second class, red in first class. On presentation, the individual tickets to and from at reduced prices and valid from the day before departure up to the day after the return will be delivered in the stations of the Eastern network to Pilgrims who have distances to travel in order to join the special train at Reims. Do not dispose of it, since on return it must again be used on the line from the east. Note well on this card the number or the letter of the compartment that each is to occupy.
2. A ticket or cardboard ticket, similar to the tickets for ordinary trips and including a round-trip ticket. Do not separate these tickets before arriving at Lourdes. This ticket will be distributed to Pilgrims only at the departure from Reims, so there is no need to claim it earlier. (As an exception it will be sent to a few Pilgrims who board en route.)

A quarter of an hour before the departure from Reims, the numbered envelopes containing the definitive tickets will be brought to each compartment of the special train. An obliging person in the compartment will be kind enough to receive and distribute them. If there was an error, please indicate this either to the inspector during the journey or to the management at the time of the first stops. The pilgrimage ticket has a true value, of which the management must give an exact accounting to the Companies. The Pilgrim who no longer has his would have to get another one and pay for it again. It is necessary, therefore, to take care not to forget it at home, lose it on the way, or let it be stolen.

Intact tickets have a right to reimbursement, but not if any part of them has been lost.—They could be taken back and reimbursed by the management to Pilgrims who are prevented from making the pilgrimage.

" *Jean !* "

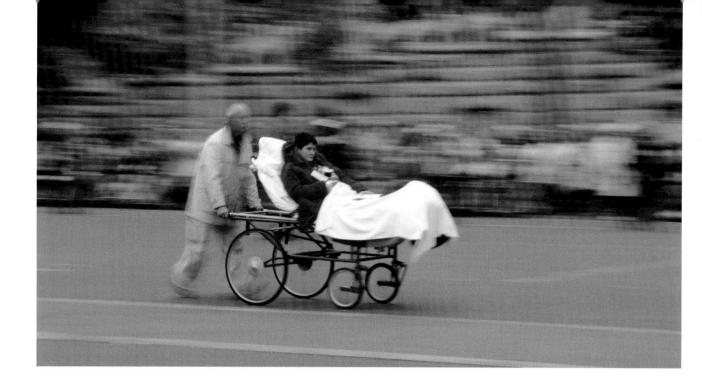

Children under the age of three years will be transported free of charge, on condition that they are held on the knees of the persons who are accompanying them; above that age, they pay the same as the adults (*Rule of the Companies*).

Companies

At the departure from Reims, stickers carrying *REIMS* and the order number for the three classes, a letter for the compartments reserved for the sick, a double letter for the second classes, will be placed outside, to the right and to the left of the compartments. It is thus easy for each Pilgrim to recognize the compartment he is to occupy. No one may change compartments without authorization from the Director.

The places inside the compartments can be neither designated nor retained; the Pilgrims must arrange that among themselves, and it is to be desired that the greatest spirit of charity and kindness preside over these arrangements. One can agree, for instance, to occupy the corners alternately.

In coach

The Pilgrims may take with them only baggage that is carried by hand and placed in the coaches.

Do not remove too much luggage or clutter compartments with trunks, boxes, and baskets that are too large to slide under the seats or hang above.

The pilgrims have no rights in the baggage car.

While the train is running, it is *rigorously* forbidden, under pain of legal prosecution, to throw out of windows empty bottles or other objects that could injure employees. The Directors of the group decline all responsibility on this subject. Be careful not to strip the station gardens.

Installation of the sick.—Compartments in sufficient numbers are reserved for patients hospitalized or admitted by the Committee. Except for rare exceptions, we must not distribute them among the nondisabled, even when these latter are their friends or their compatriots.

Stretcher-bearers

Management *alone* designates the stretcher-bearers whose mission it is to transport the sick. Nevertheless, we appeal to the goodwill of a few other nondisabled pilgrims to aid in the disembarking of the sick and in their installation into cars. 🕊

AT LOURDES

François Mauriac

Sillon de Bordeaux et du Sud-Ouest, 1905

The dawn, through the windows of the compartment, makes the flame flickering on the ceiling fade. Lourdes! … The pilgrims from Sillon descend, exhausted, and their pitiful group tramples in the mud, under a little icy rain that falls hopelessly…. But it is here that a streak of sunlight tears through the mist, the snowy peaks fade in the mist, the morning wind quickly cleans the sky and carries to us the softened echo of distant hymns. We run to the grotto where everyone is on their knees, reciting loud rosaries, and the thousands of little lights from candles flutter, barely visible in the bright daylight. At the sight of our spikes, hands stretch toward us, and the Pau, Blayais, Limousins, and Brestois comrades sport, in turn, the Le Sillon badge.

> **"Thirty thousand intoxicated and conquered men follow Jesus toward the town."**

Several hours later, thirty thousand intoxicated and conquered men follow Jesus toward the town, like the crowds of another time on the roads of Galilee, acclaiming him, imploring his pity with an infinite love. Above this ocean of inclined heads and as if carried by them, the golden monstrance comes forward, shining in the bright sun, and around it, the wind waves multi-colored banners and heavy emblazoned flags. Then, in the evening, there were fifteen thousand torches winding around the esplanade like a strange procession of glow worms, while the basilica was lit up to the top and the *Ave Marias* surged toward it with an immense clamor. Silence was established and majestically the *Credo* rose in the night. Then the crowd dispersed; it was no longer anything but a distant hum of hymns, and the last torches wandered on the black background of the earth like sparks in the ashes of half-burned paper…. The next day, Le Sillon had its true day.

While the young people of Catholic Youth and the deputy Lasies were giving very enthusiastic speeches at the palace, eighty comrades were climbing the Calvary under a fiery sun. At each station, Father Villaume, from Blaye, told us with much faith all that the painful path can inspire in a Christian of Le Sillon…. And the little troop, gathered together, rose in the fiery light toward the summit where it knelt—very far, it seemed,

the end of our fears and of our hopes with these distant comrades whom destiny had made us meet in the blessed city and whom we were going to leave that evening?... It is on this street that Germain, Darbon, Mauriac speak eloquently of Le Sillon, and also the little comrade employed at the arsenal of Brest, who tells us of his attachment to the Cause and of his great desire to make it triumph.... All that was intimate and personal. The passersby, captivated, stopped in front of these young men, who were proud to have Christ in their hearts and finding in Him an invincible force for preparing a city of justice and love.... There rose from the plain a refrain of litanies with bursts of fanfare softened by the distance, and an odor of incense traveled through the leaves of the chestnut trees.... The time came to go our separate ways. In the dying glow of the setting sun, the little road was full of sadness. We went down silently. At that time, we met Bishop Énard of Cahors, the great orator who for three days had the ardent crowd of pilgrims vibrating around his chair. He saw our spikes and said to us: "I love Le Sillon ..., tell Marc Sangnier that I have prayed for him...." Then he opened his breviary and showed us the picture of Marc

that he piously kept in it.... And our joy was increased when the Italian prelate Bishop Radini-Tedeschi of Bergamo and personal friend of Pius X, declared to those of us who had visited him that the Sovereign Pontiff loved us and blessed us. In this way the Virgin had wished to reserve in her town such encouragements for Le Sillon.

In the evening, the Sillonists from Bordeaux, kneeling before the grotto, prayed that Jesus might remain the invisible friend seated in the midst of us and that he might help us build the city dreamed of, despite the egotism and mad ignorance of the world.... Then there was the disgust of the dreary return by coach ..., the rude awakening in the brutal and monotonous life. 🕊

from the earth—around the cross that stood out, thin, against the deep sky. The last prayer over, we gaily followed the ingenious Pérotin, who intoned with his well-known conviction the song of the Young Guard; and we arranged ourselves, one above another, on the back of a hill, at the bottom of which a road passed by.... The edge of a path ... wasn't this the place chosen to cause

François Mauriac

THE GROTTO OF NAGOYA

Pierre-Marie Compagnon

Lourdes in Japan, 1909

Pierre-Marie Compagnon

In Nagoya, one of the most populous and important cities in Japan, Father Ferrand had had a beautiful grotto set up to the glory of Mary Immaculate in thanksgiving for a cure obtained following a novena to Our Lady of Lourdes.

An elderly woman, bedridden for three and a half months with severe pain in her kidneys and legs, had been able to get up after the end of the novena. On September 8, the feast of the Nativity of Mary, she made on foot the half-hour journey that separated her from the church in order to attend Mass, receive Communion, and thank her heavenly benefactress.

This sudden healing made a great impression on the Christians and on all the pagans who knew the sick woman.

The grotto was blessed on February 10, 1909, and Father Ferrand gives the following account of it:

"The new Lourdes grotto set up at Nagoya, near my chapel, was solemnly blessed by Archbishop Mugabure of Tokyo last night on February 10.

"Nearly two hundred pagans, a hundred Christians, and seven missionaries attended the ceremony. It began with a series of speeches in which the apparition and miracles of Lourdes were recounted and the glories of Mary Immaculate were celebrated. Then the procession took place on the grounds of the Catholic mission. It was 8:30 at night. Pagans and Christians mixed together, each carrying his lantern, walked in order, preceded by the cross and followed by the clergy. Going to the grotto, they sang in Japanese the litanies to the Virgin. After having passed under a gateway of greenery, at the top of which floated, surrounded by lanterns, the French and Japanese flags intertwined, we arrived in front of the grotto, and the bishop proceeded with the blessing ceremony.

"They then returned to the chapel. Evening prayer was followed by an eloquent address by the archbishop and Benediction of the Most Holy Sacrament. Nearly two hundred pagans, after having bowed before the Virgin, whose name they had perhaps heard for the first time, bowed before Christ Jesus, the one true God, whom they still did not know.

"The next morning, the anniversary of the first apparition of the Virgin at Lourdes, the archbishop celebrated the great pontifical Mass and distributed Communion to the Christians.

"The Nagoya newspapers had sent representatives. Never had this city resonated with the name of the Virgin Mary as it had these two days. Hundreds of leaflets telling the story of Lourdes had been distributed everywhere.

"Grant that the Immaculate One may become the queen of this great city of Nagoya, the fourth largest in Japan, with its population of 350,000 souls! May She finally permit me to erect soon, close to her grotto, a temple less unworthy of her and one that will become for Nagoya the beacon of truth!

"Since that time," writes Fr. Ferrand, "I have been witness to several extraordinary healings: among others, on June 23, that of the little Philomène Yokota, aged three years, daughter of one of my best Christians. Attacked by croup and in great danger, with a fever of 108 degrees, she was suddenly and completely cured after having taken some Lourdes water while her parents were reciting the rosary."

The missionary also gave thanks to Our Lady of Lourdes for the case of a pagan dying of consumption, who was completely cured after having received baptism and having drunk the water from the grotto. The whole family converted. This was at Hamamatsu, another station in Father Ferrand's district. A beautiful statue of Our Lady of Lourdes, quite recently arrived from France, is going to commemorate the memory of this miracle. It will be placed in a grotto. ❧

ENCYCLICAL LETTER ON THE PILGRIMAGE OF LOURDES

His Holiness Pope Pius XII

At Rome, July 2, 1957

To our very dear brothers Achille Cardinal Liénart, Bishop of Lille, Pierre Cardinal Gerlier, Archbishop of Lyon, Clément Cardinal Roques, Archbishop of Rennes, Maurice Cardinal Feltin, Archbishop of Paris, Georges Cardinal Grente, Archbishop-Bishop of Mans, and to all our venerable brothers, the archbishops and bishops of France, in peace and communion with the apostolic see.

Beloved Sons and Venerable Brethren, Greetings and Apostolic Benediction.

Deep in our soul are profound and pleasant memories of the pilgrimage to Lourdes which We had the privilege of making when We went to preside, in the name of Our Predecessor, Pius XI, over the Eucharistic and Marian celebrations marking the close of the Jubilee of the Redemption. We are particularly pleased, therefore, to learn that, on the initiative of the Bishop of Tarbes and Lourdes, this Marian city is preparing an appropriate celebration for the centenary of the apparitions of the Immaculate Virgin at the grotto of Massabielle and that an international committee has been set up for this purpose under the presidency of His Eminence Eugene Cardinal Tisserant, Dean of the Sacred College of Cardinals. We wish to join with you, Beloved Sons and Venerable Brothers, in thanking God for the great favor granted your country and for the many graces He has bestowed on multitudes of pilgrims during the past century. We wish to invite all Our children to renew in this jubilee year their confident and generous devotion to her who, in the words of Saint Pius X, deigned to establish at Lourdes "the seat of her immense kindness" (Letter of July 12, 1914: *A.A.S.* 6: 1914, p. 376).

Translation taken from the Vatican website: https://www.vatican.va/content/pius-xii/en/encyclicals/documents/hf_p-xii_enc_02071957_le-pelerinage-de-lourdes.html.

I

Every Christian land is a Marian land; there is not a nation redeemed in the blood of Christ which does not glory in proclaiming Mary its Mother and Patroness. This truth is brought into sharp relief by reflection on the history of France. Devotion to the Mother of God dates back to the early days of France's evangelization, and Chartres, one of the most ancient Marian shrines, still attracts a great number of pilgrims, including thousands of young people. The Middle Ages, which, especially through Saint Bernard, sang Mary's glory and celebrated her mysteries, witnessed a marvelous flowering of French cathedrals dedicated to our Lady: Le Puy, Rheims, Amiens, Paris, and so many others.... With their spires upthrust they announce from afar the glory of the Immaculate; they heighten its splendor in the pure light of their stained-glass windows and in the harmonious beauty of their statues. They bear witness above all to the faith of a people which outdid itself in a magnificent display of energy,

erecting against the sky of France the permanent homage of its devotion to Mary.

In the cities and the countryside, on the hilltops and overlooking the sea, shrines consecrated to Mary—whether humble chapels or splendid basilicas—little by little enfolded the country in their protective shadow. Princes and shepherds of souls and the faithful without number have come to these shrines through the centuries, to the holy Virgin whom they have greeted with titles expressive of their hope or gratitude. Here they invoke *Notre Dame de Miséricorde* [Our Lady of Mercy], *de Toute Aide* [of All Help], *de Bon Secours* [of Prompt Succor]. There the pilgrim seeks refuge near *Notre Dame de la Garde* [Our Lady of Watchfulness], *de Pitié*, or *de Consolation*. Elsewhere the pilgrim's prayer rises to *Notre Dame de Lumiere* [Our Lady of Light], *de Paix, de Joie*, or *d'Esperance* [of Hope]. Or he implores the intercession of *Notre Dame des Vertus, des Miracles*, or *des Victoires*. It is a wonderful litany of invocations whose unceasing recital tells, from province to province, the blessings which the Mother of God has bestowed on the land of France through the ages.

In many ways the nineteenth century was to become, after the turmoil of the Revolution, a century of Marian favors. To mention but a single instance, everyone is familiar today with the "miraculous medal". This medal, with its image of "Mary conceived without sin", was revealed to a humble daughter of Saint Vincent de Paul whom We had the joy of inscribing in the catalogue of Saints, and it has spread its spiritual and material wonders everywhere. A few years later, from February 11 to July 16, 1858, the Blessed Virgin Mary was pleased, as a new favor, to manifest herself in the territory of the Pyrenees to a pious and pure child of a poor, hardworking Christian family. "She came to Bernadette", We once said. "She made her her confidante, her collaboratrix, the instrument

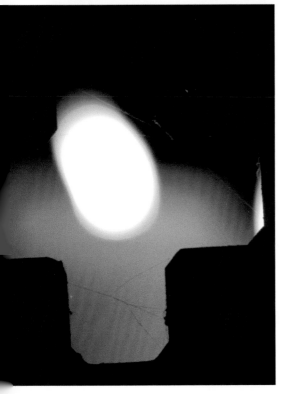

of her maternal tenderness and of the merciful power of her Son, to restore the world in Christ through a new and incomparable outpouring of the Redemption" (Discourse delivered at Lourdes on April 28, 1935: Eugenio Cardinal Pacelli, *Discorsi e panegirici* [2nd ed., Vatican, 1956] p. 435).

You are quite familiar with the events that took place at Lourdes at that time, the spiritual proportions of which are better measured

> " *Crowds flocked even then . . . into the shrine erected at Mary's request.* "

today. You know, Beloved Sons and Venerable Brethren, the astonishing circumstances under which the voice of that child, the messenger of the Immaculate, compelled the world's recognition despite ridicule, doubt, and opposition. You know the steadfastness and purity of her testimony, wisely put to the test by episcopal authority and approved as early as 1862.

Crowds flocked even then and they still surge into the grotto of the apparitions, to the miraculous spring, and into the shrine erected at Mary's request.

There is the moving procession of the lowly, the sick, and the afflicted. There is the impressive pilgrimage of thousands of the faithful from a particular diocese or country. There is the quiet visit of a troubled soul seeking truth. "No one", We once said, "has ever seen such a procession of suffering in one spot on earth, never such radiance of peace, serenity, and joy!" (ibid., 437). Nor will anyone ever know, We might add, the full sum of the benefits which

the world owes to the aid of the Virgin! "*O specus felix, decorate divae Matris aspectu! Veneranda rupes, unde vitales scatuere pleno gurgite lymphae!*" ("O blessed grotto, favored by Mary's presence! O hallowed rock whence spring the living waters of a flowing stream!"—Office of feast of the Apparitions, Hymn for II Vespers).

This century of Marian devotion has also in a certain way woven close bonds between the See of Peter and the shrine in the Pyrenees, bonds which We are pleased to acknowledge. The Virgin Mary herself desired this tie. "What the Sovereign Pontiff defined in Rome through his infallible Magisterium, the Immaculate Virgin Mother of God, blessed among all women, wanted to confirm by her own words, it seems, when shortly afterward she manifested herself by a famous apparition at the grotto of Massabielle" (Decree *de Tuto* for the Canonization of Saint Bernadette, July 2, 1933: *AAS* 25: 1933, p. 377). Certainly the infallible word of the Roman Pontiff, the authoritative interpreter of revealed truth, needed no heavenly confirmation that it might be accepted by the faithful. But with what emotion and gratitude did the Christian people and their pastors receive from the lips of Bernadette this answer which came from heaven: "I am the Immaculate Conception"!

It is therefore not surprising that it should have pleased Our Predecessors to multiply their favors toward this sanctuary. As early as 1869 Pius IX of holy memory rejoiced that the obstacles created against Lourdes by the malice of men "rendered stronger and more evident the clarity of the fact" [Letter of September 4, 1869, to Henri Lasserre: Vatican Secret Archives, *Ep. lat.* anno 1869, n. 388, f. 695]. And strengthened by this assurance, he heaped spiritual benefits upon the newly erected church and crowned the statue of our Lady of Lourdes. In 1892 Leo XIII granted the proper Office and Mass of the feast "*In apparitione Beatae Mariae*

Virginis Immaculatae", which his successor was to extend to the Universal Church a short time later. Henceforth the ancient appeal of the Scriptures was to have a new application: "Arise, my love, my beautiful one, and come. My dove in the clefts of the rock, in the hollow place of the wall" [*Cant*. 2. 13–14. Gradual of the Mass of the feast of the Apparitions]. Near the end of his life, this great Pontiff decided to install and bless a reproduction of the grotto of Massabielle in the Vatican gardens, and in those days his voice rose to the Virgin of Lourdes in an ardent and trusting prayer: "In her power may the Virgin Mother, who once cooperated through her love with the birth of the faithful into the Church, now be the means and guardian of our salvation; may she return the tranquility of peace to troubled souls; may

she hasten the return of Jesus Christ in private and public life" [Brief of September 8, 1901: 21 *Acta Leonis* XIII, 159–60].

The fiftieth anniversary of the definition of the dogma of the Immaculate Conception of the Blessed Virgin gave Saint Pius X occasion to bear witness in a solemn document to the historic connection between this act of the Magisterium and the apparitions at Lourdes. "Pius IX", he wrote, "had hardly defined it to be of Catholic faith that Mary was from her very origin exempt from sin, when the Virgin herself began performing miracles at Lourdes" [Encyclical letter *Ad diem illum*, February 2, 1904: I *Acta Pii X* 149, 22]. Soon afterward he created the episcopal title of Lourdes, attached it to that of Tarbes, and signed the introduction of the cause for the beatification of Bernadette.

It was especially reserved to this great Pope of the Eucharist to emphasize and promote the wonderful harmony existing at Lourdes between Eucharistic worship and Marian prayer. "Devotion to the Mother of God", he noted, "has led to a flowering at Lourdes of remarkable and ardent devotion to Christ our Lord" [Letter of July 12, 1914: AAS 6: 1914, p. 377]. It could not have been otherwise. Everything about Mary directs us to her Son, our only Savior, in anticipation of whose merits she was immaculate and full of grace. Everything about Mary raises us to the praise of the adorable Trinity; and so it was that Bernadette, praying her rosary before

the grotto, learned from the words and bearing of the Blessed Virgin how she should give glory to the Father, Son, and Holy Spirit. We are pleased in this centenary year to adopt as Our home the homage rendered by Saint Pius X: "The unique glory of the shrine of Lourdes lies in the fact that people are drawn there from everywhere by Mary to adore Jesus Christ in the august Sacrament, so that this shrine—at once a center of Marian devotion and a throne of the Eucharistic mystery—surpasses in glory, it seems, all others in the Catholic world" [Brief of April 25, 1911: Arch. brev. ap., *Pius X, an. 1911, Div*. Lib. IX, pars I, f. 337].

Benedict XV wanted to enrich this shrine, already loaded down with favors, with new and valuable indulgences, and though the tragic circumstances of his Pontificate did not allow him to multiply public expressions of his devotion, he nevertheless willed to honor the Marian city by granting to its bishop the privilege of the pallium at the place of the apparitions. Pius XI, who had been to Lourdes himself as a pilgrim, continued the work of Benedict XV. He had the joy of raising to the honors of the altar the girl who had been favored by the Virgin and who, in the habit of the Congregation of Charity and Christian Instruction, had become Sister Marie Bernard. Did he not, so to say, authenticate on his part the promise made by the Immaculate to young Bernadette that she would "be happy not in this world, but in the next"? From that time on, Nevers, which takes pride in keeping Bernadette's precious relics, has attracted a great number of Lourdes pilgrims who have wanted to learn from her how the message of Lourdes applies to our day. Soon the illustrious Pontiff who, like his predecessors, had honored the anniversary celebrations of the apparitions by sending a legate, decided to conclude the Jubilee of the Redemption at the Grotto of Massabielle where, in his own words, "the Immaculate Virgin Mary appeared several times to Blessed Bernadette Soubirous, and, in her kindness, exhorted all men to do penance at the scene of these wondrous apparitions, a place she has showered with graces and miracles" [Brief of January 11, 1933: Arch. brev. ap. *Pius XI*, *Ind. Perpet.* f. 128]. Truly, Pius XI concluded, is this sanctuary "now justly considered one of the principal Marian shrines in the world" [ibid.].

We could not refrain from adding Our voice to this unanimous chorus of praise. We did so particularly in Our Encyclical *Fulgens corona,* by recalling, in the spirit of Our Predecessors, that "the Blessed Virgin Mary herself wanted to confirm by some special sign the definition which the Vicar on earth of her Divine Son had pronounced amidst the vigorous approbation of the whole Church" [Encyclical letter *Fulgens corona*, September 8, 1953: *AAS* 45: 1953, p. 578. (English tr. in *The Pope Speaks*, vol. 1, no. 1, p. 43—Ed.)]. On that occasion We recalled how the Roman Pontiffs, conscious of the importance of this pilgrimage, had never ceased to "enrich it with spiritual favors and generous benefits" [ibid.]. The history of the past century, which We have recalled in its broad outlines, is a constant illustration of this Pontifical generosity, the most recent manifestation of which has been the closing at Lourdes of the centenary year of the definition of the dogma of the Immaculate Conception. But We would like especially to recall to your attention, Beloved Sons and Venerable Brothers, a recent document in which We encouraged the growth of a missionary apostolate in your beloved country. We intended by this message to call to mind the "singular merits which France had acquired through the centuries in the progress of the Catholic faith", and for this reason "We turned Our mind and heart to Lourdes where, four years after the definition of the dogma, the Immaculate Virgin herself gave supernatural confirmation to the

declaration of the Supreme Teacher, by appearances, conversations, and miracles" [Apostolic constitution *Omnium Ecclesiarum*, August 15, 1954: AAS 46: 1954, p. 567].

Today once again We turn to the famous shrine as it prepares to receive the crowds of centenary pilgrims on the shores of the River Gave. In the past century ardent public and private prayers have obtained from God many graces of healing and conversion at Lourdes through Mary's intercession, and We are firmly confident that in this jubilee year our Lady intends to respond open-handedly once more to the expectation of her children. But We are particularly convinced that she urges us to master the spiritual lessons of the apparitions

and set ourselves upon the path which she has so clearly traced for us.

II

These lessons, a faithful echo of the Gospel message, accentuate in a striking way the differences which set off God's judgments from the vain wisdom of this world. In a society which is barely conscious of the ills which assail it, which conceals its miseries and injustices beneath a prosperous, glittering, and trouble-free exterior, the Immaculate Virgin, whom sin has never touched, manifests herself to an innocent child. With a mother's compassion she looks upon this world redeemed by her Son's blood, where sin accomplishes so much ruin daily, and three times makes her urgent appeal: "Penance, penance, penance!" She even appeals for outward expressions: "Go kiss the earth in penance for sinners." And to this gesture must be added a prayer: "Pray to God for sinners." As in the days of John the Baptist, as at the start of Jesus' ministry, this command, strong and rigorous, shows men the way which leads back to God: "Repent!" [Mt 3:2; 4:17]. Who would dare to say that this appeal for the conversion of hearts is untimely today? But the Mother of God could come to her children only as a messenger of forgiveness and hope. Already the water flows at her feet: "*Omnes sitientes, venite ad aquas, et haurietis salutem a Domino*" [Office of the feast of the Apparitions, first Response of Third Nocturne]. At this spring where gentle Bernadette was the first to go to drink and wash, all miseries of soul and body will flow away. "And I went and washed and I see", the grateful pilgrim will be able to reply, in the words of the blind man of the Gospel [Jn 9:11]. But as was true for the crowds which pressed around Jesus, the healing of bodily ills is still a gesture of mercy and a sign of that power which the Son of Man has to forgive sins [cf. Mk 2:10]. The Virgin invites us to the blessed grotto in her Divine Son's name for the conversion of our hearts and in the hope of forgiveness. Will we heed her?

The true greatness of this jubilee year is in the humble answer of the man who admits that he is a sinner. Great blessings for the Church could be justly anticipated if every pilgrim to Lourdes—in fact, every Christian united in

spirit with the centenary celebrations—would first realize within himself this work of sanctification, "not in word, neither with the tongue, but in deed and in truth" [1 Jn 3:18]. Moreover, everything invites him to this work, for nowhere, perhaps, except at Lourdes does one feel so moved to prayer, to the forgetting of oneself, and to charity. When they see the devotion of the stretcher-bearers and the serene peace of the invalids, when they consider the spirit of brotherhood which unites the faithful of all races in a single prayer, when they observe the spontaneous mutual assistance and the sincere fervor of the pilgrims kneeling before the grotto, then the best of men are seized by the appeal of a life more completely dedicated to the service of God and their brothers; the less fervent become conscious of their lukewarmness and return to the road of prayer; quite hardened and skeptical sinners are often touched by grace, or at least, if they are honest, are moved by the testimony of this "multitude of believers of one heart and one soul" [Acts 4:32].

But in itself this experience of a few brief days of pilgrimage is not usually sufficient to engrave in indelible letters the call of Mary to a genuine spiritual conversion. That is why We exhort the shepherds of dioceses and all priests to outdo one another in zeal that the centenary pilgrimages may benefit by preparation, and, above all, by a follow-up which will be as conducive as possible to a profound and lasting action of grace. Only on condition of a return to regular reception of the sacraments, a regard for Christian morals in everyday life, entry into the ranks of Catholic Action and other apostolates recommended by the Church, can the great crowds expected to gather at Lourdes in 1958 yield—according to the expectations of the Immaculate Virgin herself—the fruits of salvation so necessary to mankind today.

But however important it may be, the conversion of the individual pilgrim is not enough. We exhort you in this jubilee year, Beloved Sons and Venerable Brothers, to inspire among the faithful entrusted to your care a common effort for the Christian renewal of society in answer to Mary's appeal. "May blind spirits … be illumined by the light of truth and justice", Pius XI asked during the Marian feasts of the Jubilee of the Redemption, "so that those who have gone astray into error may be brought

back to the straight path, that a just liberty may be granted the Church everywhere, and that an era of peace and true prosperity may come upon all the nations" [Letter of January 10, 1935: AAS 27, p. 7].

> *"The Virgin Mother of God, immaculate in her conception, showed herself to this very innocent young girl."*

But the world, which today affords so many justifiable reasons for pride and hope, is also undergoing a terrible temptation to materialism which has been denounced by Our Predecessors and Ourselves on many occasions. This materialism is not confined to that condemned philosophy which dictates the policies and economy of a large segment of mankind. It rages also in a love of money which creates ever greater havoc as modern enterprises expand, and which, unfortunately, determines many of the decisions which weigh heavy on the life of the people. It finds expression in the cult of the body, in excessive desire for comforts, and in flight from all the austerities of life. It encourages scorn for human life, even for life which is destroyed before seeing the light of day. This materialism is present in the unrestrained search for pleasure, which flaunts itself shamelessly and tries, through reading matter and entertainments, to seduce souls which are still pure. It shows itself in lack of interest in one's brother, in selfishness which crushes him, in justice which deprives him of his rights—in a word, in that concept of life which regulates everything exclusively in terms of material prosperity and earthly satisfactions. "And I will say to my soul. the rich man said, Soul, thou hast many good things laid up for many years; take thy ease, eat, drink, be merry. But God said to him, Thou fool, this night do they demand thy soul of thee" [Lk 12:19–20].

To a society which in its public life often contests the supreme rights of God, to a

society which would gain the whole world at the expense of its own soul [cf. Mk 8:36] and thus hasten to its own destruction, the Virgin Mother has sent a cry of alarm. May priests be attentive to her appeal and have the courage to preach the great truths of salvation fearlessly. The only lasting renewal, in fact, will be one based on the changeless principles of faith, and it is the duty of priests to form the consciences of Christian people.

Just as the Immaculate, compassionate of our miseries, but discerning our real needs, came to men to remind them of the essential and austere steps of religious conversion, so the ministers of the Word of God should, with supernatural confidence, point out to souls the narrow road which leads to life [Mt 7:14]. They will do this … without concealing anything of the Gospel's demands [cf. Lk 9:55]. In the school of Mary they will learn to live not only that they may give Christ to the world, but also, if need be, to await with faith the hour of Jesus and to remain at the foot of the cross.

Assembled around their priests, the faithful must cooperate in this effort for renewal. Wherever Providence has placed a man, there is always more to be done for God's cause. Our thoughts turn first to the host of consecrated souls who, within the framework of the Church, devote themselves to innumerable good works. Their religious vows dedicate them more than others to fight victoriously under Mary's banner against the onslaught which inordinate lust for freedom, riches, and pleasure makes on the world. In response to the Immaculate, they will resolve to oppose the attacks of evil with the weapons of prayer and penance and by triumphs of charity. Our thoughts turn also to Christian families, to ask them to remain faithful to their vital mission in society. May they consecrate themselves in this jubilee year to the Immaculate Heart of Mary! For married couples this act of piety will be a valuable aid in performing their conjugal duties of chastity and faithfulness. It will keep pure the atmosphere in which their children grow up. Even more, it will make the family, inspired by its devotion to Mary, a living center of social rebirth and apostolic influence. Beyond the family circle, professional and civic affairs offer a vast field of action for Christians who desire to work for the renewal of society. Gathered about the Virgin's feet, docile to her exhortations, they will first take a searching look at themselves and will try to uproot from their consciences any false judgments and selfish impulses, fearing the falsehood of a love for God which does not translate itself into effective love for their brothers [see 1 Jn 4:20]. Christians of every class and every nation will try to be of one mind in truth and charity, and to banish misunderstanding and suspicion. Without doubt, social structures and economic pressures of enormous weight burden the goodwill of men and often paralyze it. But if it is true, as Our predecessors and We Ourselves have insistently stressed, that the quest for social and political peace among men is, above all, a moral problem, then no reform can bear fruit, no agreement can be lasting without a conversion and cleansing of heart. In this jubilee year the Virgin of Lourdes reminds all men of this truth!

And if in her solicitude Mary looks upon some of her children with a special predilection, is it not, Beloved Sons and Venerable Brothers, upon the lowly, the poor, and the afflicted whom Jesus loved so much? "Come to me, all you who labor and are burdened, and I will give you rest", she seems to say along with her Divine Son [Mt 11:28]. Go to her, you who are crushed by material misery, defenseless against the hardships of life and the indifference of men. Go to her, you who are assailed by sorrows and moral trials. Go to her, beloved invalids and infirm, you who are sincerely welcomed and honored at Lourdes as the suffering members of our Lord. Go to her and receive peace of heart, strength for your daily duties, joy for the sacrifice you offer. The Immaculate Virgin, who knows the secret ways by which grace operates in souls and the silent work of this supernatural leaven in this world, knows also the great price which God attaches to your sufferings united to those of the Savior. They can greatly contribute, We

have no doubt, to this Christian renewal of society which We implore of God through the powerful intercession of His Mother. In response to the prayers of the sick, of the humble, of all the pilgrims to Lourdes, may Mary turn her maternal gaze upon those still outside the limits of the only fold, the Church, that they may come together in unity. May she look upon those who are in search, who are thirsty for truth, and lead them to the source of living waters. May she cast her glance upon the vast continents and their limitless human areas where Christ is unfortunately so little known, so little loved; and may she obtain for the Church freedom and the joy of being able to respond everywhere, always youthful, holy, and apostolic, to the longing of men.

"Kindly come …", said the Virgin to Bernadette. This discreet invitation, which does not compel but is addressed to the heart and requests with delicacy a free and generous response, the Mother of God addresses again to her children in France and the whole world. Christians will not remain deaf to this appeal; they will go to Mary. It is to each of them that We wish to say at the conclusion of this letter with St. Bernard: "*In periculis, in angustiis, in rebus dubiis, Mariam cogita, Mariam invoces. . . Ipsam sequens, non devias; ipsam rogans, non desperas; ipsam cogitans, non erras; ipsa tenente, non corruis; ipsa protegente, non metuis; ipsa duce, non fatigaris, ipsa propitia, pervenis …*" ["Amid dangers, difficulties, and doubts, think of Mary, invoke Mary's aid…. If you follow her, you will not stray; if you entreat her, you will not lose hope; if you reflect upon her, you will not err; if she supports you, you will not fall; if she protects you, you will not fear; if she leads you, you will not grow weary; if she is propitious, you will reach your goal…." Second Homily on the *Missus est*: PL CLXXXIII, 70–71].

We are confident, Dear Sons and Venerable Brothers, that Mary will hear your prayer and

Ours. We ask her this on the feast of the Visitation, which fittingly honors her who a century ago visited the land of France. And in inviting you to sing to God together with the Immaculate Virgin the Magnificat of your gratitude, We invoke upon you and your faithful, on the shrine of Lourdes and its pilgrims, on all those who bear the responsibilities of the centenary celebration, the most bounteous outpouring of grace. In token of which We impart with all Our heart, and with Our constant and paternal best wishes, the Apostolic Benediction.

Given at Rome, from Saint Peter's, on the feast of the Visitation of the Most Holy Virgin, July 2, 1957, the nineteenth year of Our Pontificate.

MIRACLES

LOUIS BOURIETTE

FIRST PERSON
MIRACULOUSLY HEALED

Doctor Pierre-Romain Dozous

The Lourdes Grotto, its fountain, its cures, 1874

The cures that took place at Lourdes form a long chain, whose existence I particularly noticed, its first rings having been formed before my eyes, in the very places where a mysterious being had appeared to Bernadette.

The starting point of this long chain is thus the Lourdes sanctuary. It extended from there, step by step, first into the towns surrounding the city, then into the countryside and into the neighboring departments, then into the various parts of France, and finally into all Catholic countries.

This sanctuary, so famous today, possesses, beneath the feet of the statue of the Holy Virgin, innumerable silent but irrefutable witnesses of all the extraordinary cures effected by the water from the spring: these are the memories left by invalids of every kind, freed there from the ailments that had overwhelmed them for years and against which human science had been powerless.

The cures are the cement of this vast historical edifice that is called the Lourdes affair.

I have studied it with infinite care and very great perseverance, and I declare that these are the cures that were produced at the Lourdes sanctuary, through the action of the water from the spring, which have made the supernatural character of it perfectly obvious to men of good faith.

I must admit here that, without these cures, my mind, which is little inclined to accept any miraculous explanation at all, would have yielded only with much

> **The cures are the cement of this vast historical edifice that is called the Lourdes affair.**

difficulty, even about so remarkable a phenomenon in so many ways. But the cures of which I have so often been the eyewitness and with which I am now dealing have cast a light in my mind that does not allow me to misunderstand the importance of Bernadette's visit to the caves of Massabielle and the reality of the apparitions with which she was favored. These cures, poorly accepted, I know, by the people determined to oppose the events that occurred in Lourdes, cannot, however, be seriously contested. We ask the opponents only to be willing to study them with us.

Created at the Massabielle grottos, the immense work whose beginning I have seen, which I have followed through all the obstacles that have vainly opposed it, which I have seen reach a truly surprising greatness, occupies at this moment the entire world and will occupy it always since it has a foundation in common with that of the Catholic religion itself, of which it is only a special manifestation and a perceptible demonstration, through all the miraculous cures that are ceaselessly being produced before the Lourdes sanctuary.

The first event of this kind that was presented to my observation was that of Louis Bouriette, quarryman from the city of Lourdes.

One day in the year 1858, shortly after the events occurred in the Massabielle grottos, as I was crossing one of the city boardwalks, twenty-five men of all ages, gathered into a group, stopped me to talk about the numerous cures worked by the water of Bernadette's spring. I listened attentively to these men, very surprised at all their stories. Soon Louis Bouriette joined us, saying to me:

"I am convinced that all these men are telling you about the marvelous cures that the water from the grotto produces every day."

"Yes, Louis, I replied to him. And these stories seem so strange to me that I consider them fairy-tales."

"Well! If you are incredulous on that point, please listen to me: You undoubtedly remember the terrible accident of which I was the victim many years ago and the wound in my right eye that made me blind. Well! This eye, thanks to the water from the spring at the Massabielle grottos, has regained its power, completely annihilated for a long time. Now it perceives objects as perfectly as the left eye."

Surprised by Louis Bouriette's declaration, fearing that he wanted to take pride in a miracle invented for his own pleasure, I said to him:

"That is what we are going to see."

And after having put a blindfold over his left eye, I stood about twenty paces from my man; then I made all sorts of movements with my hands, which Louis Bouriette distinguished completely. After that, going closer to him, I wrote in pencil a few lines on my notebook, which he deciphered without difficulty. These two very conclusive experiences threw me into the greatest astonishment; I then asked Louis Bouriette, in the presence of the twenty-five men who had kept me close to them, what he had done to obtain such a result.

"As soon", he told me, "as Bernadette had made flow from the bottom of the grotto the spring that cured so many sick people, I wanted to use her water to cure my right eye. One day when my whole family was going out to the fields, I kept my younger daughter close to me; I gave her the bottom of a bottle and sent her to the Massabielle grottos so that she would fill it with water, still muddy, provided by the spring

When I had possession of this water, I began to pray. . . .

discovered by Bernadette. When I had posses-sion of this water, I began to pray, and, address-ing Our Lady of the Grotto, I humbly begged her to be willing to be with me while I washed my right eye with the water from her spring. Immediately I wet the lost eye several times in a row with this heavily soggy mud that was in the bottom of the bottle. After having finished these ablutions and my prayer, I looked around me, attentively and using both eyes at once, at all the objects that were in my room. They seemed to me more distinct than before that process. Then I closed my left eye so as to use only the right, which, to my great surprise, had regained its visual faculties. I washed it again several times within a short period of time, and my vision, after these various washes, was what it is at this time, excellent."

After this very important account, I exam-ined both eyes of Louis Bouriette, which, in their form and the organization of their vari-ous parts, did not seem to be any different. The pupils of both eyes functioned consistently when exposed to light. In the lower part of the right eye, there was a very obvious scar where the circumference of the transparent cornea met the sclera in an area of a little over one-third of an inch. It was the only trace that remained on this organ of the action of the injuring agent that had attacked it.

The restoration of vision in the right eye, which had been deprived of it for more than twenty years, is a fact of the greatest impor-tance, which obliges me to make known in all its details the observation concerning Louis Bouriette, so that the impartial reader, in appreciating the power of the wounding agent, the gravity of the disorders that it had pro-duced, might at the same time appreciate, too, the power of the healing agent used by Louis

" *When the sick hurried*
in the footsteps of the
Divine Master, a great number
of them rose again cured. "

Bouriette. This man, a quarryman, was one day occupied with his brother, Joseph, with loading a blast hole. During this dangerous operation, they had the misfortune of doing something that set the powder on fire. The violent explosion that was produced around the two brothers led to Joseph's sudden death. Louis, violently knocked down on the body of his brother, remained unconscious for more than two hours, his hands and face horribly burned. The bodies of the two unfortunate quarrymen were carried into their house, where Louis immediately received all that his condition required.

This unfortunate man was attacked by a violent meningitis (inflammation of the lining of the brain), accompanied by a delirium that made him very dangerous. In order to restrain him and to keep those who were caring for him safe from any accident, I was obliged to have him put in a straitjacket.

The cerebral illness lasted three months; the burns on his face and hands disappeared rather quickly.

When Louis seemed sufficiently healed to leave his house and resume his work as a quarryman, he was struck by a nervous agitation that obliged him to lead a wandering life for two years.

After this period, this man, who had become calmer, seriously sought work.

One day, when he wanted to engage in stonecutting and to do some difficult work, he noticed that his sight perceived objects of small dimensions in so confused a way that it was impossible for him to do this kind of work. He then came to my house to ask me to examine his eyes and to determine if they were functioning correctly, using all the means in my power.

I examined his eyes, and I easily saw that the right eye had been injured at the bottom of the circumference of the transparent cornea, at the point of juncture with the sclera; that the pupil was strongly dilated, very insensitive to the action of light; that, whatever position one had Louis Bouriette take, in whatever setting of light one established, the vision was excessively weak; and when one wanted the perception of objects to take place through the simultaneous use of both eyes, great confusion reigned, proving the inequality of the visual power of the two eyes.

I did not leave unknown to the quarryman what was for me the gravity of the lesion of the right eye and the certitude I had that the amaurosis, which already existed almost completely, would soon become definitive, despite whatever the treatments that might be used to try to cure it.

Despite this prognosis, Louis Bouriette insisted in a particular way that I work actively to treat it.

After a thousand fruitless attempts, I finally made Louis Bouriette understand that the functions of vision had been lost on his right side and that he had to deal with it.

The poor quarryman resumed his ordinary work as actively as he could, having only the use of his left eye. He thus came to the period of the events at the Grotto and finally found in the water from the spring the remedy that medical science had not given him.

The accident that had happened to Louis Bouriette was so serious that everyone must have thought that death would follow. The strength of his constitution and the treatments used preserved him from that end which many people had thought inevitable.

But the amaurosis of the right eye, the result of a wound to the transparent cornea by the impact of a little fragment of stone and the considerable weakening of nerves imprinted on the eyeball, was not curable by any means at the disposition of human science.

The shock produced by the violence of the blow to this organ had attacked the whole

nervous system, especially the retina, in a way that led to the weakening of vision and soon to amaurosis.

It is invariable, and science is settled on this point,[1] that every time an eye is struck by an object large or small, thrown by dust, even when it only skims the surface in passing, it experiences a concussion that is always enough to lead to an incurable amaurosis.

It very often happens that the other eye, which could not escape the action of the concussion produced because of the relationship of the nerves that exists between the two eyes, ends, in its turn, being weakened and seems also to be affected by amaurosis.

I must sincerely admit that this healing of Louis Bouriette produced a profound emotion in me. I see in this first event the revelation of truths that I was still far from suspecting.

From that moment on, I attached myself in a very particular way to the sick, who came by the hundreds, especially on transferred feast days, like Corpus Christi, in front of the Massabielle rocks, in order to obtain there the healing of reputedly incurable ills.

I am going to cite, among the events that were offered in great number to my observations, several that most deserve to fix the attention of the reader. 🕊

Pierre-Romain Dozous

---

1. Boyer, *Traité de chirurgie*; Magendie, *Précis élémentaire de physiologie*; Devergie, *Médecine légale*.

PIERRE DE RUDDER

MIRACULOUSLY HEALED AT LOURDES . . . A BELGIAN!

Joris-Karl Huysmans

Les foules de Lourdes, 1906

And I tell myself that the Virgin of Lourdes is disconcerting, for the counterfeits are worth as much as the original, are sometime even more active and produce more miracles.

The history in Belgium of the sanctuary of Oostackker, located in a village in the midst of the Slootendriesch park, three miles from Gand, is singular to say the least. It began with a social project with which the Virgin had nothing to do. In 1870, the taste for aquariums was fashionable among the rich families of the Belgian people; a marquise of Courtebourne, who owned the Slootendriesch castle, got it into her head to go build one, and since an aquarium cannot do without a fake cave, she also decided to build one of those. After the placement in her park was chosen, the work began; in the meantime, the parish priest of Oostakker, Father Moreels, showed an image of the Lourdes grotto to the Marquise and persuaded her to reserve in the cemented pile of its rockeries a niche in order to place there a statue of the Immaculate Conception, copied from the one in the Pyrenees. All was finished in 1871; and three years later, the few peasants from the hamlet who were coming to pray before the aquarium, and the Virgin, had given rise, without anyone quite knowing how, to thousands of visitors. It grew to ten thousand in one day, and the miracles exploded. The first that was recorded dates from February 12, 1874; this fell to Mathilde Verkimpe, a child ten years old, living in Loochristi. She was crippled, unable to walk without crutches; all the doctors in the hospitals of Gand had declared themselves powerless to cure her. Her mother went to ask for her healing at the grotto, brought back water from Lourdes that was distributed there, and, during a novena, she rubbed the

> ## *It began with a social project with which the Virgin had nothing to do.*

leg of her daughter with this water; and, at the end of the novena, the little one was instantaneously cured and was able to go on foot to thank the Virgin.

And the miracles continue: people usually make a habit of going around the grotto three times; they rinse themselves with water that has fallen into a basin from the aquarium, into which, every morning, a few drops from the Lourdes spring have been thrown, and the most diverse diseases, such as coxalgia and blindness, disappear as soon as this liquid touches them.

In the month of May in the year 1875, in order to answer the needs of the pilgrims, a Gothic-style church, without a transept, with two steeples, was built; service of the pilgrimage was entrusted to the Jesuit Fathers from the Belgian and Oostakker province that had become famous in Flanders. Thousands of candles are burned there, as in Lourdes, and pyramids of votive offerings rise up, above the grotto, into the trees.

It was in this place that the most extraordinary healing ever observed in the memory of man appeared.

On February 16, 1867, a peasant by the name of Pierre de Rudder, residing in Jabbeke, a village located near Bruges, had his left leg broken by a falling tree; there was a fracture of the tibia and the fibula, and bone fragments were so numerous that when the leg was moved, you heard, according to the expression of the doctor who first cared for him, the bones rattling, like hazelnuts in a bag; when these fragments were removed from the tissue, you could discern in the wound the two bones that remained intact, at a distance of a little over an inch from each other.

They were not familiar with antisepsis at that time, and no matter how hard they tried to use solid bandages, the juncture of the two bones, which were bathed in pus, never formed; the lower part of the member, no longer welded to the other, tossed about like a rag, in every sense.

The surgeons, who came one after another to the unfortunate man, declared the case incurable, and Professor Thiriart, from Brussels, who was consulted as a last resort, proposed amputating the leg. De Rudder refused; and, for more than eight years, he suffered atrocious torture, obliged several times a day to dress this wound whose pus knew no bounds, and dragging himself along as best he could on crutches.

He had heard of Oostakker; he resolved to go there to ask the Virgin for his healing. On April 7, 1875, three men hoisted him onto the train leaving for Gand; when he got off in this city, he was carried in the Oostakker omnibus, and his leg, as well wrapped up as possible, let out streams of fluid and blood that filtered through the cloth and stained the seat; when he arrived in front of the statue of the Virgin, he rested a little, drank a sip of water, and then wanted to follow the custom of making a tour of the grotto three times. Supported by his wife, he succeeded in making this tour twice, and, at the end of his strength, he fell, exhausted, onto a bench. He begged Our Lady of Lourdes to save him, and he suddenly lost his head, did not know where he was, found himself, in regaining consciousness, in front of Her, on his knees, and he rose, cured. No more hole, the bones were joined tougher; he did not even limp, for the two legs were of equal length. This miracle created an

enormous stir in Flanders; twenty-two doctors were occupied with it; meticulous investigations were made, aimed at more impartiality on the part of both Catholics and the incredulous; all the practitioners who had cared for him, all the people of the village of Jabbeke who had seen the condition of the wound on the day of his departure, all those who had been present at the miracle were questioned; de Rudder was subjected to the most rigorous examinations; it was very necessary to agree about the authenticity of this unprecedented event, of a wound cured all on its own, in a second, and of a bone fragment a third of an inch long, destined to replace the one that was missing, grown instantaneously, following a prayer.

He remained upright on the leg, a bluish spot at the place where the break had been, as if to attest that they had not been the toy of an illusion, that the rupture had indeed existed.

Twenty years went by, with that leg never having weakened or having been, from the point of view of solidity, inferior to the other, and de Rudder, suffering from pneumonia, died at the age of seventy-five, on March 22, 1898. On May 24 of the following year, they proceeded to do an autopsy of his leg.

We see that the Virgin does not play the difficulty, as one says in the game of billiards; she replaced this leg just as the most skilled surgeon would have done if the operation had been possible; and she made it possible by the immediate suppression of a purulent center and by the spontaneous creation of a bone.

This autopsy of a miracle is certainly the most extraordinary proof that could ever be furnished here below as a remedy for human impotence in healings. Zola's nerve injuries, autosuggestion, faith that heals, all the old nonsense of the Salpêtrière and Nancy schools, are thus reduced to nothing.

AUTOSUGGESTION

Émile Zola

Lourdes, 1894

"I told you that I had become a believer—nevertheless, to speak the truth, I understand very well why this worthy Doctor Bonamy is so little affected and why he continues calling upon doctors in all parts of the world to come and study his miracles. The more doctors that might come, the less likelihood there would be of the truth being established in the inevitable battle between contradictory diagnoses and methods of treatment. If men cannot agree about a visible sore, they surely cannot do so about an internal lesion the existence of which will be admitted by some, and denied by others. And why then should not everything become a miracle? For, after all, whether the action comes from nature or from some unknown power, medical men are, as a rule, none

the less astonished when an illness terminates in a manner which they have not foreseen. No doubt, too, things are very badly organized here. These certificates from doctors whom nobody knows have no real value. All documents ought to be stringently inquired into. But even admitting any absolute scientific strictness, you must be very simple, my dear child, if you imagine that a positive conviction would be arrived at, absolute for one and all. Error is implanted in man, and there is no more difficult task than that of demonstrating to universal satisfaction the most insignificant truth."

Pierre[1] had now begun to understand what was taking place at Lourdes, the extraordinary spectacle which the world had been witnessing for years, amidst the reverent admiration of some and the insulting laughter of others. Forces as yet but imperfectly studied, of which one was even ignorant, were certainly at work—autosuggestion, long-prepared disturbance of the nerves; inspiriting influence of the journey, the prayers, and the hymns; and especially the healing

Translation by Ernest A. Vizetelly, from Émile Zola, *The Three Cities: I, Lourdes*, vols. 1 and 2 (Macmillan, 1897; New York: Grosset & Dunlop, n.d.), pp. 270–72.

1. The hero of the book, Father Pierre Froment, serves as a common thread for the three novels by Émile Zola, *Lourdes*, *Rome*, and *Paris*.

breath, the unknown force which was evolved from the multitude, in the acute crisis of faith. Thus it seemed to him anything but intelligent to believe in trickery. The facts were both of a much more lofty and much more simple nature. There was no occasion for the Fathers of the Grotto to descend to falsehood; it was sufficient that they should help in creating confusion, that they should utilize the universal ignorance. It might even be admitted that everybody acted in good faith—the doctors void of genius who delivered the certificates, the consoled patients who believed themselves cured, and the impassioned witnesses who swore that they had beheld what they described. And from all this was evolved the obvious impossibility of proving whether there was a miracle or not. And such being the case, did not the miracle naturally become a reality for the greater number, for all those who suffered and who had need of hope? Then, as Doctor Bonamy, who had noticed that they were chatting apart, came up to them, Pierre ventured to inquire: "What is about the proportion of the cures to the number of cases?"

"About ten percent," answered the doctor; and reading in the young priest's eyes the words that he could not utter, he added in a very cordial way: "Oh! There would be many more, they would all be cured if we chose to listen to them. But it is as well to say it, I am only here to keep an eye on the miracles, like a policeman as it were. My only functions are to check excessive zeal, and to prevent holy things from being made ridiculous. In one word, this office is simply an office where a visa is given when the cures have been verified and seem real ones. 🐦

Émile Zola

FAITH HEALING

Jean-Martin Charcot

"Bibliothèque diabolique" Series, 1897

The *New Review*, taking text from a recent trip by a famous writer to a religious shrine and discussions that were raised on that occasion, is asking my opinion about *faith healing*. The question is not one of those that could leave me indifferent. It is, moreover, of interest to any doctor, since the essential goal of medicine is the healing of the sick no matter what healing process is implemented. In this order of ideas, faith healing seems to me to be the ideal to be attained, since it often works when all the other remedies have failed. That is why, for a long time, when faced with certain specific cases, I have sought, after many others, to penetrate, as much as possible, the mechanism of its production so as to utilize its power, and it is the opinion that I have formed under these conditions that I am going to explain in a few words.

I would add that in such a matter, as in any other, it is necessary never to depart from the rigor inherent in the scientific discussion; impassioned controversies serve no purpose but to confuse and compromise the best causes. It is not by affirmations without proof or by baseless denials that one can hope to resolve this question of faith healing, which, I repeat, belongs entirely to the scientific order, where occurrences that are well and entirely studied, grouped together in conclusion, are the only arguments that can be admitted. The occurrences that, in my already long special practice, I have had the occasion to observe are not isolated, far from it, for faith healing and its result, the miracle—without attaching to this word any other meaning than that of a healing effected outside the means ordinarily used by clinical medicine—respond to a category of actions that do not escape the natural order of things. The therapeutic miracle has its determinism, and the laws that preside at its genesis and at its evolution begin to be, on more than one point, sufficiently known for the group of occurrences that are included under this term to appear with a look that is special enough not to escape our appreciation completely. There is, moreover, reason to congratulate ourselves, since by understanding more

> *It is necessary never to depart from the rigor inherent in the scientific discussion.*

clearly these determinations, we increasingly place at our disposal the great resources of faith healing, and, by that fact, the illness finds us less and less disarmed before it.

It is the elements themselves of this determinism that we are going to study. Their grouping will lead us to a conclusion that I can, moreover, give immediately. The healing, of a particular appearance, the direct product of faith healing, that is commonly called in therapeutics by the name of miracle is, as can be demonstrated, in the majority of cases, a natural phenomenon that has been produced in all times, in the midst of the most varied civilizations and religions, the most dissimilar in appearance, just as at present it is observed at all latitudes. The occurrences said to be miraculous, and I do not claim to express anything very new here, have a twofold character: they are created by a special disposition of the patient's mind; a confidence, a credibility, a suggestibility, as they say today, constitutive of the faith healing whose setting into motion is of a variable order. On the other hand, the domain of faith healing is limited; in order to produce its effect, it must be addressed to cases whose healing requires no other intervention than this power that the mind possesses over the body, of which Dr. Hack Tuke has given, in his beautiful book[1] such a remarkable analysis. No intervention is likely to free it from its limitations, for we can do nothing against natural laws. We have never noted, for example, in examining compilations dedicated to so-called miraculous healings, that faith healing made an amputated limb grow back. On the other hand, we find hundreds of healings of paralysis, but I believe that these have always been of the nature of those that Professor Russel Reynolds[2] qualifies by the general term of paralyses "dependent on idea".

Jean-Martin Charcot

1. *Illustrations of the Influence of the Mind upon the Body in Health and Disease Designed to Elucidate the Action of the Imagination* (London: Churchill, 1872).

2. *Remarks on Paralysis and Other Disorders of Motion and Sensation Dependent on Idea*, read to the medical section of the British Medical Association, Leeds, July 1869, in *British Medical Journal*, November 1869.

Offert par une dame Italienne

ce monument veut dire:

Retrouver la Foi c'est plus
que retrouver la Vue.

> *Healing requires no other intervention than this power that the mind possesses over the body.*

OFFICE OF MEDICAL OBSERVATIONS

Gustave Boissarie

Upon entering the Office of Medical Observations what strikes us first of all is a prominent inscription that reminds us that "the first transcripts written at the dictation of patients without sufficient means of control cannot offer guarantees that only later investigations must give them. Illnesses and cures are left to study, to discussion."

If we wanted to take into account the reservations that we never cease to formulate, all the legends that prevail about Lourdes would vanish on their own. Nervous illnesses, suggestion, reduced to their real proportions, would no longer serve as themes that are obsolete and a hundred times refuted.

We know how to take into account suggestion, whose field constantly shrinks around us. Under the eyes of often incredulous colleagues, our conclusions are severely controlled.

In reading our transcripts, our readers will be able to understand the importance of the cures that we have observed.

They will also see that the number of doctors attending the meetings of the Office of Medical Observations, far from decreasing, seems to increase every year, and we find on our lists a greater number of medical professors and celebrities of all kinds.

We write down 130 to 150 transcripts every year. And these transcripts are far from representing the total number of cures that are produced around the grotto. In 1905, we had registered five cures for the pilgrimage from Lyon, and the report published by the director indicates 58 cures and improvements.[1]

For the pilgrimage from Arras, we had retained two observations, and the Arras account indicated six other cures and several great improvements.

The pilgrimage from Metz had left two cures on our registers, while in the *Bulletin de Metz*, we read about twenty-two of them.

It is the same for all the pilgrimages; according to this calculation, we would hardly have in our transcripts even one-tenth of the cures that are produced, and again we must observe that a great number of cures are not published, are obtained in the numerous Lourdes sanctuaries spread around the entire world, following novenas, with water from the

---

1. In 1908 we had not written down any cure on our registers for the Lyon pilgrimage, and the official report indicated 52 of them.

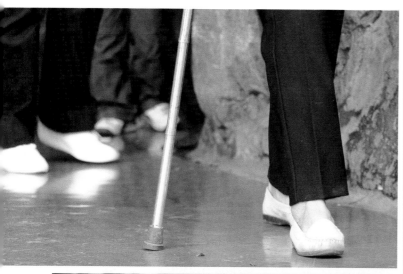

" In the footsteps of the Divine Master "

grotto, and we do not know about these cures.

Putting all these facts together, we arrive at 1,000 or 1,500 cures a year.

When the sick hurried in the footsteps of the Divine Master, a great number of them rose again cured. The Gospel preserves for us the account of only a small number of these cures.

At Lourdes, we can only glean in a field too vast for our glance to be able to embrace it in its entirety. We preserve only the account of the most significant facts that are reported to us.

On our transcripts, we have about a third from organic diseases: wounds, tumors, bone decay, cancer, and lung disease in the last stage.

Cures of functional disorders are often confined to organic lesions and then have to be ranked with the former. There are others, on the other hand, that clearly fall into the category of nerve damage.

There are some cases that are doubtful or difficult to classify. Finally, there are some observations that must be removed from our statistics. Among the cures of organic illnesses, we have some cures of cancer.

A doctor leads his wife in prayers of thanksgiving. She was cured of breast cancer on December 8, although two professors on the faculty wanted to do an immediate and total removal of the right breast. At the end of a novena, the whole tumor had disappeared.

The novena had begun on November 30; the fifth day, the tumor began to get smaller, and her general condition was improving. On December 8, only a small, absolutely painless lump remained, and her health seemed entirely restored. 🐦

Gustave Boissarie

A NOVELIST ON THOSE WHO HAD BEEN CURED

CLÉMENTINE TROUVÉ
BEFORE ÉMILE ZOLA

Georges Bertrin

Historical review of the events of Lourdes, apparitions and cures, 1905

In 1892 a very well-known novelist went to Lourdes at the time of the great pilgrimages. He wished to see what was taking place, and to give his own version of it.

But he was one of those men who do not leave their interests or their fame to fate. He took every means to prepare public opinion. The papers were primed with his confidences, and the world impatiently looked forward to the book which was to air his views.

At Lourdes, every door was opened to the writer, and he was allowed to see everything. It was made a point of honor that this should be the case. Especially was he given access to the Medical Office during the consultations, a permission which is not always easily obtained during the crowded season by one who is not a doctor. There he met many who had been cured. He questioned them at his leisure, and had several interesting discussions with the doctors who were present, and many of whom were as skeptical as himself.

Nay, more. He first saw them in the pilgrims' train, that *white train* he has so wonderfully described with his realistic pen, as fond of pain as of vice.

We give here the principal figures he tried to make live again in his work. It will be interesting to compare truth with fiction.

CLÉMENTINE TROUVÉ

On August 20, 1892, there were assembled in the Medical Office at Lourdes several doctors, journalists, and M. Zola.

Translation taken from George Bertrin, *Lourdes: A History of Its Apparitions and Cures*, trans. Mrs. Philip (Agnes Mary Rowland) Gibbs (New York: Benziger, 1928), pp. 185–91.

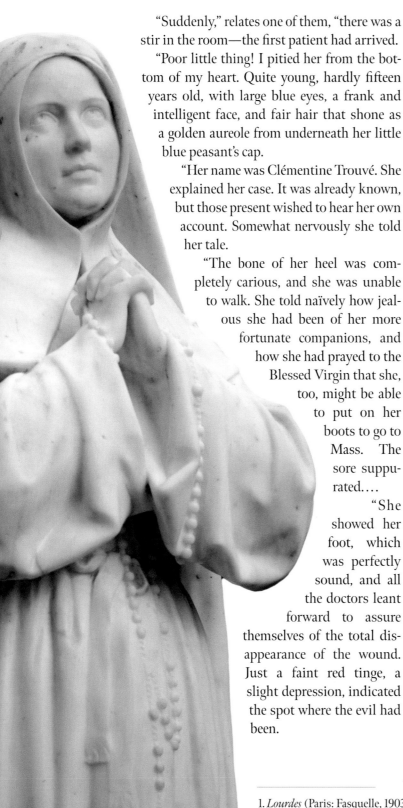

"Suddenly," relates one of them, "there was a stir in the room—the first patient had arrived.

"Poor little thing! I pitied her from the bottom of my heart. Quite young, hardly fifteen years old, with large blue eyes, a frank and intelligent face, and fair hair that shone as a golden aureole from underneath her little blue peasant's cap.

"Her name was Clémentine Trouvé. She explained her case. It was already known, but those present wished to hear her own account. Somewhat nervously she told her tale.

"The bone of her heel was completely carious, and she was unable to walk. She told naïvely how jealous she had been of her more fortunate companions, and how she had prayed to the Blessed Virgin that she, too, might be able to put on her boots to go to Mass. The sore suppurated....

"She showed her foot, which was perfectly sound, and all the doctors leant forward to assure themselves of the total disappearance of the wound. Just a faint red tinge, a slight depression, indicated the spot where the evil had been.

"M. Zola, who was present, bit the tip of his glove, a sign with him of mental discomfiture. The girl was in a hurry to be off. They let her go at length. She hurriedly put on her boot and stocking, and was gone like a bird, impatient to be beyond the range of all those eyes watching her every movement."

The novelist, who in his book called *Clémentine Trouvé* Sophie Couteau, wrote:—

"All at once, a smiling, modest-looking young girl, whose clear eyes sparkled with intelligence, entered the office....

"'Tell the gentlemen how it happened, Sophie.'

"The little girl made her usual pretty gesture as a sign to everybody to be attentive. And then she began. 'Well, it was like this; my foot was past cure. I couldn't even go to church any more, and it had to be kept bandaged because there was always a lot of matter coming from it. M. Rivoire, the doctor, who had made a cut in it so as to see inside it, said that he should be obliged to take out a piece of the bone, and that, sure enough, would have made me lame for life. But when I got to Lourdes, and had prayed a great deal to the Blessed Virgin, I went to dip my foot in the water, wishing so much that I might be cured that I did not even take the time to pull the bandage off. And everything remained in the water. There was no longer anything the matter with my foot when I took it out.'"[1]

I

This M. Rivoire was, in real life, Dr. Cibiel of Lusignan (Vienne), who, having long attended the little patient, gave the following certificate:—

---

1. *Lourdes* (Paris: Fasquelle, 1903), pp. 191–92; English trans., pp. 164–65.

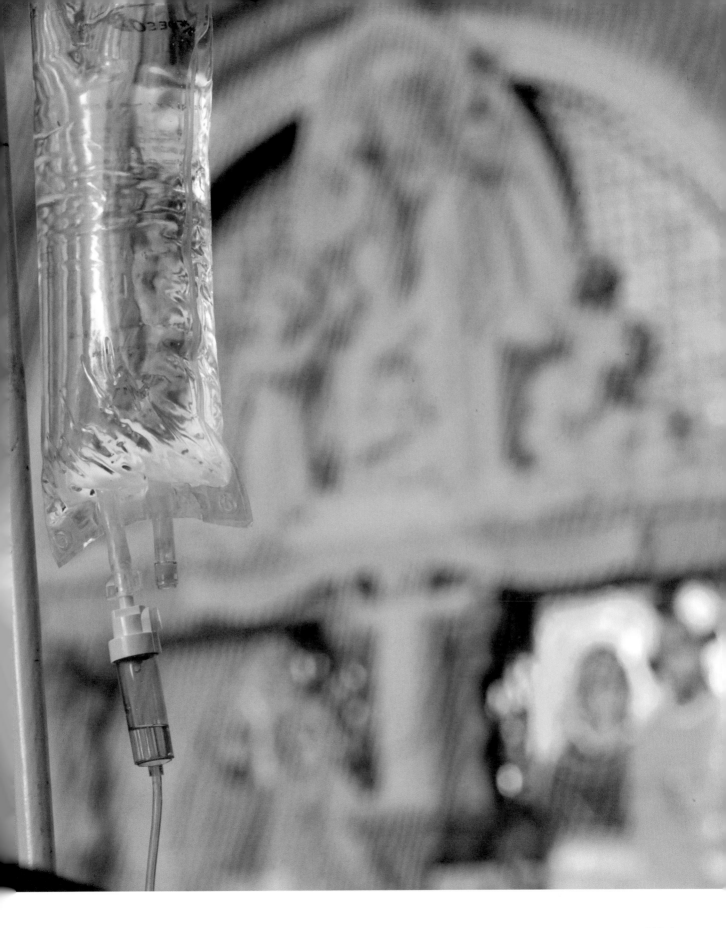

The undersigned doctor certifies that young Clémentine Trouvé, of Rouille, suffers from osteoperiostitis of the calcaneum, which has resisted treatment by incision and detergent injection. This disease can only be amenable to a radical operation on the part diseased, or to a long treatment based on local antiseptics and general analeptics.

Dr. Cibiel
Lusignan, June 11, 1891

Clémentine had reached Lourdes on August 20, 1891, with the National Pilgrimage. The next day, the 21st, her foot, which had been diseased for three years, was bathed in the piscina, and, *instantaneously*, the disease disappeared, and she was cured. There was no more suppuration, no more pain, the sore was closed, and the little girl could walk like all other children of her age. She was even able immediately to put on some boots that a lady brought for her. The sight of these boots filled her with childlike joy, and she jumped about happily when going up the stairs in the hospital.

As the journey had caused the leg to suppurate more abundantly than usual, the linen and the lint she had taken with her threatened to give way, and she said to the Viscountess de Roederer with charming ingenuity: "The Blessed Virgin was very kind to cure me on the first day, for tomorrow I should have run out of linen."

On the 22nd the news was conveyed to her doctor by M. le Curé, of the parish of Rouille.[2]

Dr. Cibiel was at Bagnols in Orne. On his return to Lusignan, eight days after, he saw his little patient, and gave her the following certificate:

The undersigned doctor certifies that Clémentine Trouvé, who has been suffering since June 12, 1891, from periostitic fistula, of tuberculous origin, in the sole of her foot, is at present cured, and does not show any more trace of her

---

2. Rouille is a market town in Vienne and near Lusignan.

old [affliction], than some scars and a slightly increased development of the sole of the foot. He, moreover, certifies that any pressure at this point is not painful, and the little invalid can stand comfortably on the bad foot.

Dr. Cibiel.
Lusignan, *Sept. 1, 1891*

When signing this certificate, Dr. Cibiel said to M. le Curé at Rouille: "I am giving you the certificate you desire with the same sincerity that I gave the certificate stating the disease."

"And when I asked him," relates the curé, "if he could not add that it was at Lourdes that the child was cured, he replied: 'No, you have witnesses to prove that. That is sufficient.'"

"'Besides,' he added, 'you will pardon me, M. le Curé, but I will say to you what I said to Mme. Trouvé, "Whether by devil or the good God, the child is cured and well cured, and I am pleased—very pleased." ' "[3]

All the inhabitants of the little village were not so pleased. The Protestants particularly were in a very bad temper.

"When I left for Lourdes," the child related a year after at the Medical Office, every one said: 'Ah! you may go on a pilgrimage, but you will return like the others,' and they mentioned a young girl of the neighborhood who had not been cured the year before.

"When I returned, and they saw me walking without crutches and cured, they all said, 'She was never ill.'"

This tale was told by Clémentine before M. Zola, who was apparently much interested.

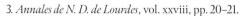

3. *Annales de N. D. de Lourdes*, vol. xxviii, pp. 20–21.

"But, doctor," he said at length to M. Boissarie, with the embarrassment of a man who can find nothing to say, "this is miraculous. I regret to see no professors of the Paris School here."

"I also," replied the doctor; "they have only to come—our doors are always open."

We may as well remark by the way that there were at this moment in the room a surgeon from a Paris hospital, some corresponding associates of the Academy of Medicine, several late house-surgeons, and some who were still practicing in the Parisian hospitals; also doctors from many of the largest French towns, from watering-places, and from foreign faculties.[4]

"Did you see the wound yourself before the cure?" asked the novelist.

"No," replied the president; "I only saw it an hour after, when the scar was still fresh. But a number of people did see it—her doctor to begin with, who certainly is not a believer. You have read his certificate."

"I wish you had seen it."

"But we cannot see all the patients that arrive in Lourdes. A thousand came yesterday. How could we investigate a thousand cases in a day? Besides, we should be accused of partiality either because of public malignity or because the rapid examination of an unknown patient could hardly be absolutely safe. We always refer first to the patients' doctors, whatever their convictions. Then if a cure is effected, we make a thorough inquiry in the person's home. This seems the best and surest method, besides, it is the only one possible.

"I make you an offer, M. Zola: will you take me at my word? There is a little girl who for three years suffered from a suppurating sore in the heel until August 21st last, on which day she was suddenly cured. Will you join with me in a scientific inquiry into these two facts, the disease and the cure? Do you accept?"

Thus publicly challenged, the novelist replied that he had not the time, that he was not able to indulge in such research. In a word, he excused himself, and said:

"As you did not see the wound yourself, show me something else, doctor."

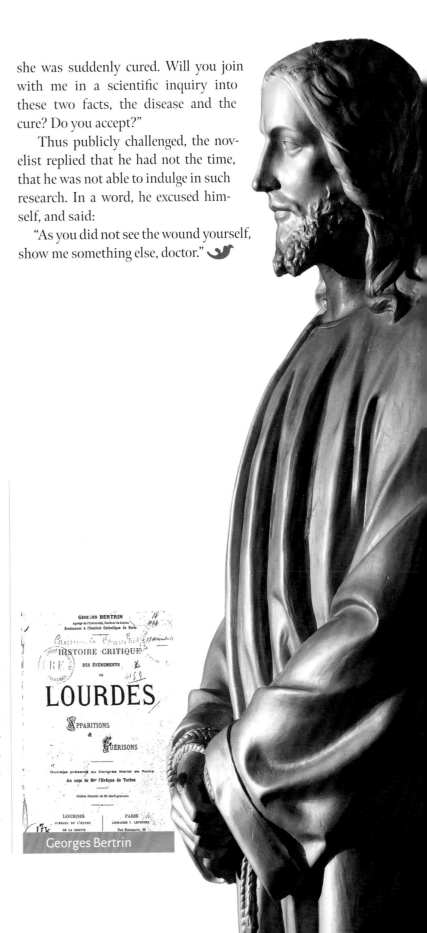

4. The names of all these doctors are given in the Office Register.

STRETCHER-BEARER

André Rebsomen

Souvenirs d'un brancardier de Lourdes, 1937

The first time I went to Lourdes, the first time I made contact with the Holy City, was in the month of August 1891. I went there with my mother; I was twenty-one years old; my law studies were completed.

A Christian education had trained me well in piety, but neither my religious sentiments nor my imagination could have given me in advance any idea of what I was going to see.

We arrived on one of the national pilgrimage trains that included that year some 20,000 pilgrims of whom 995 were sick. The spiritual regulation of the car had made me understand a little that I was entering into a still unsuspected pious atmosphere. At that time, the pilgrimage trains went at a hopelessly slow speed, and their numerous and prolonged stops easily allowed the integral application of the journey's regulation. It was already an excellent formation in one of the qualities of the true pilgrim: patience.

When we arrived in Lourdes, my mother and I found a modest lodging at the home of a brave woman who ran one of the stores on the Place Monseigneur Laurence, then called the Place de la Merlasse. The lots that are located south of this public street and on which these stores were built are called "benches of the Grotto" because in other times the women who sold objects of piety were lined up seated on the benches, a little like the sellers of candles installed today on the opposite side. The "Benches" have become houses and stores without, however, changing their name. The ground still belongs to the city, which rents it at a very good price, by auction and for a period of fifteen years. The income forms a third of the municipal revenue. But the contractors are now forbidden to give hospitality to the pilgrims in their outbuildings so as not to prejudice the interests of the hotel owners and landlords.

Barely settled in, I went to the Office of Stretcher-Bearers of Hospitality; I had no letter of recommendation. The head stretcher-bearer looked me up and down with his stern gaze; it is probable that my expression seemed sufficiently reassuring to him; he accepted me and gave me a pair of braces. I started my service immediately: I was assigned to the Reserve.

The Reserve was then installed under one of the arcades of the large ramp of the Esplanade on the Gave side, where the Office of Hospitality is now built.

The arcade was open: large green tarpaulins had been stretched there, secured with ropes, and thus forming a shelter, open only on the Gave side. All the stretchers, carried by hand or in wagons drawn by horses, were deposited in the Reserve, which served as a control station. From the Reserve, the stretcher-bearers then carried the stretchers, according to need, either to the Grotto or to the pools. Toward the end of the service and at the return time, if that was necessary, the Reserve brought the last stretchers back to their hospital.

My first impressions were intense; I will never forget them. For the first time, I was in contact with suffering, and what suffering! What a painful spectacle were these emaciated figures, these twisted limbs, these looks that were anguished and yet full of confidence and patience, of these "abridged versions of all human misery", as Bossuet said. 🐦

*" **For the first time, I was in contact with suffering.** "*

ANDRÉ REBSOMEN

SOUVENIRS
D'UN BRANCARDIER
DE LOURDES

EDITIONS «ALSATIA» PARIS
1, rue Garancière (6ᵉ)

André Rebsomen

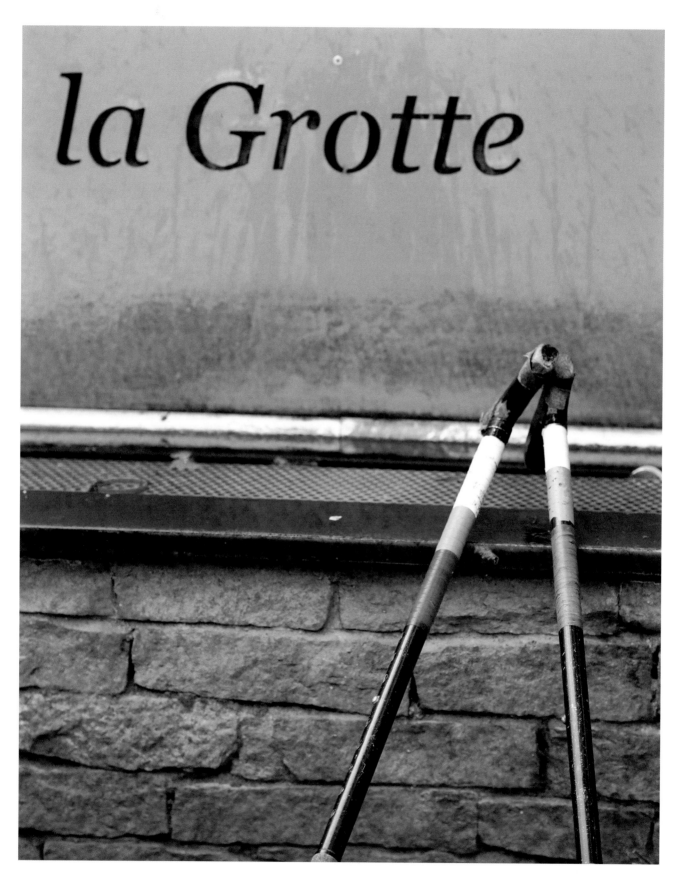

la Grotte

LOURDES DURING THE WAR

Bishop François Schœpfer

Pastoral Letters, 1921

Nevertheless, as if to give us in advance a sure pledge of this final and decisive success, Our Lady of Lourdes did not disdain curing, among others—for the eternal confusion of her German detractors—"one of the French soldiers whose bones had been broken by them". Let us note, moreover, that this prodigious healing took place following lotion made with water from the Massabielle grotto. Now certain Germans, in order to make it understood that the Immaculate Virgin had abandoned us, were saying that the spring had dried up after the beginning of the war.

The account of this healing was written by the Sister of Nevers who, at the Asile Notre-Dame de Lourdes (supplementary hospital no. 32), cared for the fortunate beneficiary of the merciful intervention of Bernadette's heavenly Lady. Following the *Annales de Notre-Dame de Lourdes* (June-July 1919 issue), we will in our turn do our duty to reproduce it as

well as a note from Dr. Paulouch, one of the majors at Hospital 32, where this soldier was being treated:

"It was—writes Sister Mathilde—during the first months of the war. Among the seriously wounded who had arrived at the hospital of Asile de Notre-Dame de Lourdes to be hospitalized there was a soldier named Colin, originally from the Ardennes, whose soul was as sick as his body."

Now his body was very much so. For, following a fracture of the upper part of the humerus, he had had several secondary hemorrhages that had seriously weakened him. In the meantime, gas gangrene had been diagnosed. The doctor tried a thermocautery incision without success. The patient was *lost*. The Sister asked him if he wanted to receive the Last Sacraments. "No!" he responded in a tone that allowed no reply. Without being discouraged, his nurses began to pray and asked Our Lady of Lourdes to wish to cure, apart from his body, the soul of this unfortunate one. They asked him again the next day, and now Colin, to everyone's surprise, accepted the help of religion and even had something torn up that he had written asking to be buried without religious ceremony.

Yet his condition was getting worse day by day. He was *abandoned by the doctor*. A new hemorrhage occurred. His blood, after having soaked his bed, had gone through the mattress and run down to the floor, all decomposed. They did not dare redo his dressing or change it for fear of hastening his death. So as to avoid contagion to the other patients and to disinfect the room, where that odor of gangrene made the air unbreathable, they transported him to the morgue. A coffin was there, all ready to receive the body as soon as the last breath was taken; and they waited from one moment to the next for the fatal outcome to transfer him immediately to the cemetery.

The Sister, however, full of confidence, began to make a novena to *Our Lady of Lourdes* for him, and the Poor Clares were asked to please join it. The dressing was undone, without any hemorrhage: it was filled with worms and exhaled an odor so foul that the nurse who was helping Sister had to put a cotton balls in her nose. They soaked the *compresses with water from the Grotto, which they also gave to the patient to drink.*

The next day, the Sister, to her profound surprise, noticed an improvement in the condition of the wound as well as in the general condition of the patient. She spoke to the major, who responded, with an incredulous air: "Bah!" The day after that, the improvement was more noticeable. Again, she advised the doctor of it, who, this time, replied: "I am going to see him." He examined him and, later, on his return, noted the improvement. All danger had disappeared. As the novena proceeded, the improvement increased, the fracture healed, and, several days later, the patient was transported to the hospital of the Assumption for the extraction of the shrapnel that had nearly caused his death.

Once healed, he was discharged, though weakness and a little functional disability remained in his arms.

He went to work in Paris in a business house where he was accepted nearly out of charity. But, little by little the condition of his arm improved so well that he could soon provide his service very well. Later, the family of his employer, having come on pilgrimage to Lourdes, brought the Sister who had cared for him a note from him, written with his injured hand, in which he expressed to her his sincere gratitude and his faith in Our Lady of Lourdes. ꙮ

> *The family of his employer ...*
> *brought the Sister ... a note from him,*
> *written with his injured hand, in which*
> *he expressed to her ... his faith in*
> *Our Lady of Lourdes.*

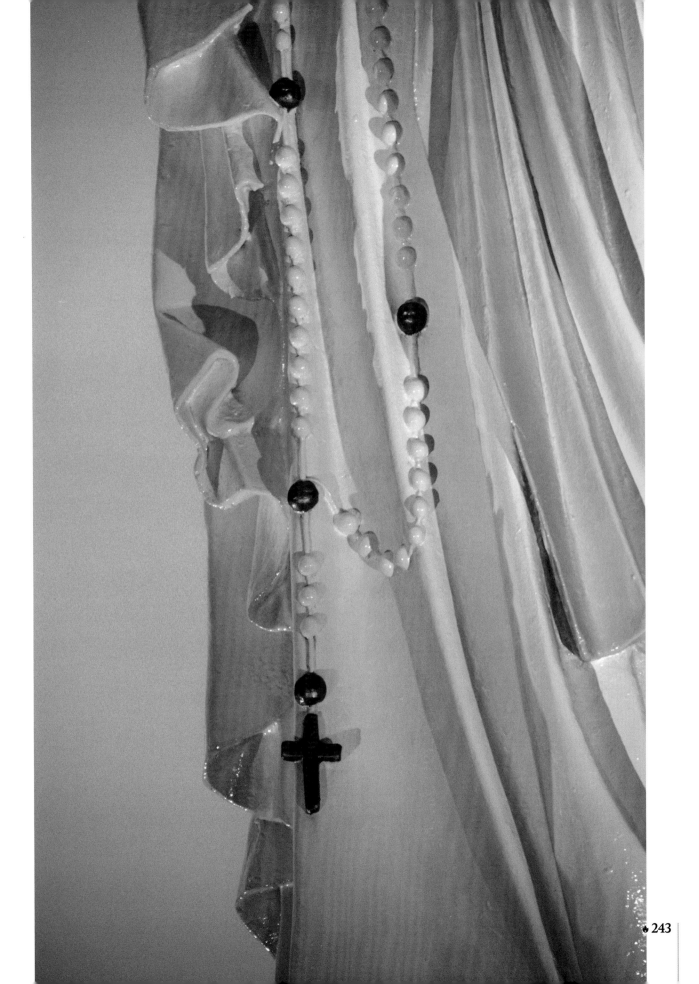